THE WAY
PEOPLE
LIVE

Life Under the

Taliban

Titles in The Way People Live series include:

Cowboys in the Old West
Games of Ancient Rome
Life Aboard the Space Shuttle
Life Aboard the Space Station
Life Among the Aztecs
Life Among the Great Plains Indians
Life Among the Ibo Women of Nigeria
Life Among the Inca
Life Among the Indian Fighters
Life Among the Pirates
Life Among the Puritans
Life Among the Samurai
Life During the American Revolution
Life During the Black Death
Life During the Crusades
Life During the Dust Bowl
Life During the French Revolution
Life During the Gold Rush
Life During the Great Depression
Life During the Middle Ages
Life During the Renaissance
Life During the Roaring Twenties
Life During the Russian Revolution
Life During the Spanish Inquisition
Life in a Japanese American Internment
   Camp
Life in a Medieval Castle
Life in a Medieval Monastery
Life in a Medieval Village
Life in America During the 1960s
Life in an Amish Community
Life in a Nazi Concentration Camp
Life in Ancient Athens
Life in Ancient China
Life in Ancient Egypt
Life in Ancient Greece
Life in Ancient Rome

Life in a Wild West Show
Life in Berlin
Life in Castro's Cuba
Life in Charles Dickens's England
Life in Communist Russia
Life in Genghis Khan's Mongolia
Life in Hong Kong
Life in Moscow
Life in the Amazon Rain Forest
Life in the Australian Outback
Life in the Elizabethan Theater
Life in the Hitler Youth
Life in the Negro Baseball League
Life in the Stone Age
Life in the Warsaw Ghetto
Life in Tokyo
Life in War-Torn Bosnia
Life of a Medieval Knight
Life of a Nazi Soldier
Life of a Roman Gladiator
Life of a Roman Slave
Life of a Roman Soldier
Life of a Slave on a Southern Plantation
Life on Alcatraz
Life on a Medieval Pilgrimage
Life on an African Slave Ship
Life on an Everest Expedition
Life on a New World Voyage
Life on an Indian Reservation
Life on Ellis Island
Life on the American Frontier
Life on the Oregon Trail
Life on the Pony Express
Life on the Underground Railroad
Life Under the Jim Crow Laws
Life Under the Taliban

THE WAY PEOPLE LIVE

Life Under the
Taliban

by Gail B. Stewart

LUCENT BOOKS

An imprint of Thomson Gale, a part of The Thomson Corporation

THOMSON

---✦---

GALE

Detroit • New York • San Francisco • San Diego • New Haven, Conn. • Waterville, Maine • London • Munich

THOMSON
✶
GALE
™

© 2005 Thomson Gale, a part of the Thomson Corporation.

Thomson and Star Logo are trademarks and Gale and Lucent Books are registered trademarks used herein under license.

For more information, contact
Lucent Books
27500 Drake Rd.
Farmington Hills, MI 48331-3535
Or you can visit our Internet site at http://www.gale.com

LIBRARY OF CONGRESS CATALOGING-IN-PUBLICATION DATA

Stewart, Gail B., 1949–
    Life under the Taliban / by Gail B. Stewart.
       p. cm. — (The way people live)
Summary: Discusses the history of Afghanistan, the rise and fall of the Taliban, and daily life under the regime.
Includes bibliographical references and index.
    ISBN 1-59018-291-X (hard cover : alk. paper)
    1. Afghanistan—History—1989–2001—Juvenile literature. 2. Afghanistan—Social conditions—Juvenile literature. 3. Taliban—Juvenile literature. I. Title. II. Series.
    DS371.3.S75 2004
    958.104'6—dc22

                           2004010378

Printed in the United States of America

Contents

Discovering the Humanity in Us All

Books in The Way People Live series focus on groups of people in a wide variety of circumstances, settings, and time periods. Some books focus on different cultural groups, others, on people in a particular historical time period, while others cover people involved in a specific event. Each book emphasizes the daily routines, personal and historical struggles, and achievements of people from all walks of life.

To really understand any culture, it is necessary to strip the mind of the common notions we hold about groups of people. These stereotypes are the archenemies of learning. It does not even matter whether the stereotypes are positive or negative; they are confining and tight. Removing them is a challenge that is not easily met, as anyone who has ever tried it will admit. Ideas that do not fit into the templates we create are unwelcome visitors—ones we would prefer remain quietly in a corner or forgotten room.

The cowboy of the Old West is a good example of such confining roles. The cowboy was courageous, yet soft-spoken. His time (it is always a he, in our template) was spent alternatively saving a rancher's daughter from certain death on a runaway stagecoach, or shooting it out with rustlers. At times, of course, he was likely to get a little crazy in town after a trail drive, but for the most part, he was the epitome of inner strength. It is disconcerting to find out that the cowboy is human, even a bit childish. Can it really be true that cowboys would line up to help the cook

on the trail drive grind coffee, just hoping he would give them a little stick of peppermint candy that came with the coffee shipment? The idea of tough cowboys vying with one another to help "Coosie" (as they called their cooks) for a bit of candy seems silly and out of place.

So is the vision of Eskimos playing video games and watching MTV, living in prefab housing in the Arctic. It just does not fit with what "Eskimo" means. We are far more comfortable with snow igloos and whale blubber, harpoons and kayaks.

Although the cultures dealt with in Lucent's The Way People Live series are often historically and socially well known, the emphasis is on the personal aspects of life. Groups of people, while unquestionably affected by their politics and their governmental structures, are more than those institutions. How do people in a particular time and place educate their children? What do they eat? And how do they build their houses? What kinds of work do they do? What kinds of games do they enjoy? The answers to these questions bring these cultures to life. People's lives are revealed in the particulars and only by knowing the particulars can we understand these cultures' will to survive and their moments of weakness and greatness.

This is not to say that understanding politics does not help to understand a culture. There is no question that the Warsaw ghetto, for example, was a culture that was brought about by the politics and social ideas of Adolf

Hitler and the Third Reich. But the Jews who were crowded together in the ghetto cannot be understood by the Reich's politics. Their life was a day-to-day battle for existence, and the creativity and methods they used to prolong their lives is a vital story of human perseverance that would be denied by focusing only on the institutions of Hitler's Germany. Knowing that children as young as five or six outwitted Nazi guards on a daily basis, that Jewish policemen helped the Germans control the ghetto, that children attended secret schools in the ghetto and even earned diplomas—these are the things that reveal the fabric of life, that can inspire, intrigue, and amaze.

Books in The Way People Live series allow both the casual reader and the student to see humans as victims, heroes, and onlookers. And although humans act in ways that can fill us with feelings of sorrow and revulsion, it is important to remember that "hero," "predator," and "victim" are dangerous terms. Heaping undue pity or praise on people reduces them to objects, and strips them of their humanity.

Seeing the Jews of Warsaw only as victims is to deny their humanity. Seeing them only as they appear in surviving photos, staring at the camera with infinite sadness, is limiting, both to them and to those who want to understand them. To an object of pity, the only appropriate response becomes "Those poor creatures!" and that reduces both the quality of their struggle and the depth of their despair. No one is served by such two-dimensional views of people and their cultures.

With this in mind, The Way People Live series strives to flesh out the traditional, two-dimensional views of people in various cultures and historical circumstances. Using a wide variety of primary quotations—the words not only of the politicians and government leaders, but of the real people whose lives are being examined—each book in the series attempts to show an honest and complete picture of a culture removed from our own by time or space.

By examining cultures in this way, the reader will notice not only the glaring differences from his or her own culture, but also will be struck by the similarities. For indeed, people share common needs—warmth, good company, stability, and affirmation from others. Ultimately, seeing how people really live, or have lived, can only enrich our understanding of ourselves.

Back to the Dark Ages

At first, the dust was all people could see—a whirling brown sandstorm rushing toward the center of the village. Soon it was obvious that the dust was being kicked up by a little pickup truck—a white Toyota with six young men riding in the back. Though the setting was southwest Afghanistan, a landlocked nation in central Asia, the truck had been painted with English slogans with the sound of American culture: "Murder Crew" on one side and "City Boys" on the other.

The men in the truck looked different from the other men of the village, too. Instead of wearing the light-colored robes and caps designed to keep people cool in the one-hundred-degree summer heat, the men in the truck were wearing jet black robes with matching silky black or white turbans. The men's turbans had long tails that ran almost to their ankles. These men were Taliban, members of the government that had taken control of most of Afghanistan.

"I Thought I Had Been Bitten by a Snake"

When the truck stopped, the Taliban jumped out and approached a group of people shopping at the bazaar, or market. They looked menacingly at the shoppers, who instinctively huddled together. The Taliban men were looking for women walking alone, a violation of a new national law that prohibited women from leaving their homes unless accompanied by a male relative as a chaperon, or *mahram*.

Zoya, a young Afghan woman, was in the bazaar with her friend Abida when the Taliban arrived. Zoya was not concerned at first because the two women were accompanied by a *mahram*, as ordered. However, she was surprised when she was singled out for punishment by one of the men:

> We had not walked very far . . . when I heard a whistling sound very close to me and, a fraction of a second later, felt a sting on my hand. I thought I had been bitten by a snake, but when I turned I saw one of the Taliban with a lash in his hand. "Prostitute!" he shouted at me, the spittle spraying his greasy beard. "Cover yourself and go from here! Go to your house!"[1]

Abida quickly apologized to the men and quietly explained to Zoya that her hand must have been visible as her robe moved while she was walking. A woman who exposed any skin at all was breaking a law, too—punishable by a public whipping. "Please be as careful as you can," Abida whispered. "We can't afford to draw any attention to ourselves."[2] Afterward, Zoya realized that she was lucky to have received only one lash with the whip. Afghan women were often given severe beatings for such infractions. In fact, in a nearby village a twelve-year-old girl who was wearing nail polish (also forbidden) was spotted by Taliban members, who used their knives to cut off her fingertips.

Afghanistan in the Dark Ages

The Taliban government, which stormed to power beginning in 1994, introduced a whole new code of laws into Afghan society. Many new laws banned common, mundane activities or customs. For example, no longer was dancing or listening to music allowed. In fact, mothers were not even allowed to sing to their children. Kite flying, a favorite pastime, was banned. Television and computer use were forbidden, too, as was the celebration of most holidays.

Some of the new laws were anything but trivial, however. Many of the harshest ones affected women. Women were required to wear a burka, a long, pleated, baglike garment that covers every inch of a woman's body—even her face. Women could not work, and they could not appear in public without a male relative. They could not receive medical care from a male doctor. Finally, neither women nor girls were allowed to attend school.

The penalties for breaking these laws were as inhumane as the laws themselves.

Women wearing burkas that cover their entire bodies beg outside a Kabul mosque. The fundamentalist Taliban regime severely punished women who exposed any part of their bodies in public.

The Taliban routinely carried out public beatings, amputations, and executions for various criminal acts. One observer noted that the coming of the Taliban was the equivalent of Afghanistan being "plunged into the Dark Ages."[3]

It is difficult to imagine life under such brutal conditions. For millions of Afghans, the new rules resulted in such poverty that life was little more than trying to find enough food for their children or protection from the hot summer sun or the frigid winter winds. And although many thousands of people did not survive the regime—those who were executed or succumbed to starvation and disease—millions did. The story of life in Afghanistan under the Taliban is not only evidence of some people's cruelty but also a reminder of the strength of the human will to survive.

The Land of the Great Game

Even before the arrival of the Taliban government, Afghanistan was a troubled land. One of the key reasons is its location in south-central Asia. Afghanistan lies at the crossroads of two important trade routes—one between Europe and China and one between India and central Asia. Over the past two thousand years, Afghanistan has been invaded many times by nations eager to control and profit from those routes. As one historian notes, "Afghanistan is a land on everyone's way to someplace else."[4]

Hard to Hold

But as desperate as other nations were to control the region that is now Afghanistan, they were not able to hang on to it. Over the centuries many strong foreign armies invaded the region, only to lose it. Alexander the Great, the world's most successful invader, marched his armies into the country in 329 B.C. He conquered much of the area but could never subdue the various tribes in Afghanistan; within a century, the Greek presence there was gone.

Alexander was followed by a host of others—from the Arabs in A.D. 652, who brought Islam to the area, to the Mongol invader Genghis Khan in the thirteenth century, Afghanistan was the site of invasions and bloody wars. And although many invaders left their mark on Afghanistan, they were all repelled.

One reason for the inability of invaders to control Afghanistan is the land itself. About the size of Texas, Afghanistan is a land of stark contrasts. Two-thirds of the region is made up of massive mountain ranges, the largest being the Hindu Kush, a Himalayan network of ranges with many peaks more than twenty thousand feet above sea level. In addition to the terrain itself being difficult, the weather in the mountains can be brutal. Winter storms blowing through the mountain passes have killed many foreign soldiers unprepared for the bitter cold.

Conversely, the deserts of southern Afghanistan are no less brutal to those unaccustomed to scorching temperatures—often more than 110 degrees Fahrenheit. Although foreign armies find it difficult to negotiate the rugged terrain—mountains in the north, deserts in the south, and rocky caves that honeycomb the central part of the country—native Afghans are well adapted to the changes in weather and know how to move through the land more easily.

"A Lot of Rubbish Left Over"

Another reason Afghanistan has been impossible for invaders to hold is the nature of its people. Afghanistan is unlike many other countries whose populations are similar in cultural and ethnic makeup. Because the mountainous terrain makes travel difficult, Afghanistan's local peoples have retained distinct ethnic or tribal identities—and collectively have rarely shown allegiance to any national leaders or central government. Any invaders trying to work out lasting treaties or agreements with Afghanistan would have found the task impossible because, in reality, there were no people who considered themselves purely "Afghans."

By far, the majority of Afghans are Pashtuns, who live in the southern and eastern parts of Afghanistan. The Pashtuns have always been the most powerful tribe and consider themselves the true Afghan people. Other tribes, although not as powerful, control the areas in which they live. The Hazaras control the mountainous regions of central Afghanistan, the Tajiks the mountains of the

northeast, the Turkmen and Kirghiz—both nomadic tribes—control the Wakhi in the north, and so on. Each tribe speaks a different language, and the tribes themselves are divided into various regional subgroups, which are led by tribal chieftans.

The history of Afghanistan is filled with hostility—not only against foreign invaders but also among the tribes themselves. An old man of Afghanistan shared with author Ahmed Rashid the myth about how God created Afghanistan and its people, who can rarely agree on anything: "When Allah had made the rest of the world, He saw that there was a lot of rubbish left over, bits and pieces and things that did not fit anywhere else. He collected them all together and threw them

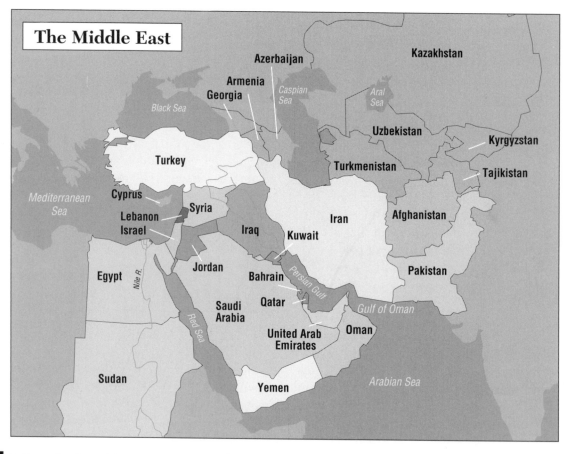

British soldiers prepare for battle with Afghan tribes in 1879. Throughout the nineteenth century, Great Britain and Russia vied for control of central Asia.

down on to the earth. That," he explained, "was Afghanistan."[5]

The Great Game

Afghanistan's invaders came and went, even in modern times. In the nineteenth century, Britain and Russia struggled for control of central Asia. Britain already controlled India and hoped to extend that control into nearby Afghanistan. By doing so, the British could en-

sure that the trade route between India and Europe stayed safe. However, Russia had other plans for India. In addition to the money to be made controlling India's trade, Russia was eager to push its influence southward to a warm water port. To do that, Russia would need to control Afghanistan. The rivalry between Britain and Russia—each trying to broaden and improve its colonial holdings—became known as the Great Game.

Britain tried establishing control in Afghanistan by a combination of diplomacy

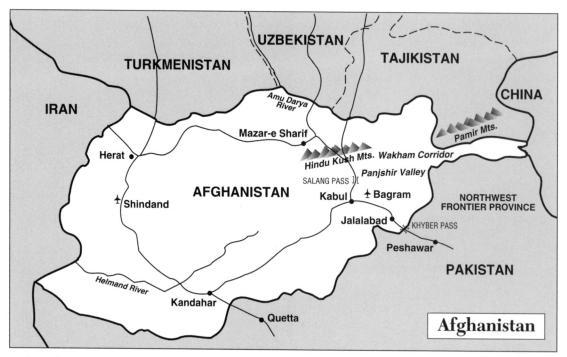

Afghanistan

and military intervention. First, British troops invaded and occupied the country; then British diplomats befriended several powerful tribal leaders and set up a puppet regime in Afghanistan that would be loyal to the British Crown. Although the method was successful at first, tribes not included in the new regime fought the new government. When Britain brought in additional forces to aid the Afghan government in fighting the rebels, many British thought the fighting would be over quickly. Considering the size and sophistication of Britain's army and weapons, the wars should have been completely one-sided.

However, the British were no match for the Afghan rebels. In 1842 tribal armies defeated the British in a war so brutal it was later dubbed "Britain's Kabul Catastrophe." One British writer noted at the time that Britain had underestimated the lengths to which the Afghan tribes would go to keep outsiders from taking over:

Across the length and breadth of the land, history . . . was written in characters of blood. Afghans were still a nation of fierce Mohammedans [Muslims], of hardy warriors, of independent mountaineers, still a people not to be dragooned into peace or awed into submission by a scattering of foreign bayonets and all the pagaentry of a puppet King.[6]

Massacre

The British army's retreat in January 1842 demonstrated how fierce the Afghan fighters were with their razor-sharp knives and outdated rifles. As the convoy of four thousand British soldiers and twelve thousand camp followers (including women and children) moved slowly from Kabul south toward a British fort in Jalalabad, the tribes opened fire from behind rocks. Anticipating the arrival of the convoy, the British set great bonfires to guide it to the safety of the fort. Of the sixteen thousand British, only one man—bleeding and hysterical—arrived in Jalalabad. It was the bloodiest defeat in all of British history.

Between 1842 and 1919, the British launched two more invasions of Afghanistan, but neither was successful. The hostility of the Afghan tribes toward foreign invaders—as well as their talent for guerrilla warfare in the most rugged climates and terrains—was too powerful an enemy.

The British writer Rudyard Kipling, in an 1892 poem called "The Young British Soldier," gave advice to anyone unlucky enough to be sent to fight in Afghanistan:

> When you're wounded and left on Afghanistan's plain,
>
> And the women come out to cut up your remains
>
> Roll to your rifle and blow out your brains.[7]

Russia in Afghanistan

In 1921 the British finally stopped trying to control Afghanistan. However, over the following years Russia (now the Soviet Union) began to establish a presence in the country. By supplying the now-independent Afghanistan with weapons and financial aid, the Soviets were able to gain influence with Afghan president Mohammed Daoud's government in Kabul.

By 1977, however, Daoud had changed his mind about the likelihood of running Afghanistan as a Communist country. He was sure that the tribal nature of Afghanistan would prevent the kind of strong central government needed for communism to be successful. Daoud tried to break ties with the Soviet Union.

Realizing that that their influence in Afghanistan was quickly disappearing, the Soviets arranged for an overthrow of Daoud's government. On April 17, 1978, the Soviets arranged for the president, along with thirty members of his family, to be assassinated. Immediately afterward, the Soviets installed a new president in Afghanistan—Nur Mohammed Taraki, who was willing to work with the Soviet Union. This violent change of government was known as the April Revolution.

"The Effect Was Catastrophic"

When the new Communist regime was in place in Kabul, Taraki and his government set to work establishing various reforms. One example was a program to redistribute farmland more equitably among the Afghan people. Anyone with more than six acres of land for grazing or farming was required to give some of it to people without land.

Many Afghan people were vehemently opposed to such reforms. They saw communism as a system that threatened the traditional ways, and even more important, they knew that one characteristic of communism was its view that religion was unnecessary. Although Afghan tribes disagreed about a great many things, they were almost all Muslim, and their religion was vital to their way of life.

Reforms such as the banning of marriage dowries threatened a number of key Muslim traditions. Another change that was particularly upsetting to many Afghans was the new flag introduced by the Communists—the traditional Islamic green flag was changed to the shade of red on the Soviet flag. According to historians Richard and Nancy Newell, to the Afghan people, it seemed that within just a few weeks their society was being turned upside down: "Any one of these programs,

Soviet tanks roll into Kabul in early 1980. The Soviet Union sent thousands of troops to Afghanistan to defeat the mujahideen rebels that threatened the newly installed Communist government.

tactlessly introduced, would almost certainly have aroused a bitter reaction among most segments of the population. When they were introduced together as a package under the red banner of communism, the effect was catastrophic."[8]

The Birth of the Mujahideen

Tribal forces began rebelling against the new government, and many government workers sent out into the countryside to begin the new reforms were killed. To combat the unrest,

the government began imprisoning Muslim clergy, student protesters, and others who were critical of the new policies. At the center of the resistance movement were conservative Muslims whose main goal was to restore Afghan society to Islam rather than allow it to be influenced by the Soviets. These Muslims were called mujahideen, word meaning "people fighting a holy war." The mujahideen believed that fighting for their religion would bring them great favor from God, or Allah.

President Taraki called on Afghanistan's army to fight the rebelling tribes. Some soldiers felt disloyal by firing on members of their tribe and deserted the army. By fall 1979 more than twenty thousand Afghan citizens had been killed, and the nation was in chaos. The Soviet Union knew the government could not survive in Afghanistan without military intervention. On December 27, 1979, ignoring the lessons of the British and others who had tried invading the region, Soviet leader Leonid Brezhnev ordered five thousand troops to Kabul. Within a week there were fifty thousand additional troops, and by February 1980 the number had risen to ninety thousand.

"Like Nailing Jelly to a Wall"

Although their numbers were impressive, their firepower was truly amazing. The Soviet army in Afghanistan had hundreds of attack helicopters, parachute battalions, and eight armored tank divisions. The mujahideen, on the other hand, were armed with old shotguns and rifles left over from the war against Britain. What should have been a quick victory, however, turned into a Russian quagmire. For one thing, superior weaponry did not prove to be a major advantage. Ironically, the mujahideen weakness—their lack of military bases, their outdated weapons, and the fact that their command structure was divided among at least ten factions—made it difficult for the Soviets to know where to attack. "Fighting Afghans," observes writer Sebastian Junger, who spent time with the mujahideen, "was like nailing jelly to a wall; in the end there was just a wall full of bent nails."[9]

In addition to being confused by its unstructured enemy, the Soviet army was young

The Toughest People on Earth

In his book *Soldiers of God: With Islamic Warriors in Afghanistan and Pakistan*, Robert D. Kaplan explains how the primitive weapons and physical toughness of the mujahideen reminded him more of ancient fighters than modern guerrilla soldiers.

"While the Soviets waged a twenty-first-century war, the Afghans fought a nineteenth-century one. The Afghans were able to survive and drive out the Soviets precisely, and only, because they were so primitive. High birth and infant mortality rates in an unforgiving mountain environment, where disease was rife and medical care absent, had seemed to accelerate the process of evolution in rural Afghanistan, making the inhabitants of the countryside—where most of the [mujahideen] came from—arguably the phsyi-cally toughest people on earth. They could go for long periods of time without food and water, and climb up and down mountains like goats. Keeping up with them on their treks and surviving on what they survived on reduced me and other Westerners to tears. They seemed an extension of an impossible landscape that had ground up one foreign invader after another.

The [mujahideen] borrowed little from other modern guerrilla struggles. They had a small number of vehicles and, until the later stages of the war, few walkie-talkies, leaving the enemy without communications to intercept. Like the ancient Greeks, the [mujahideen] used runners to carry messages between outposts. . . . Predicting the [mujahideen's] actions was like forecasting the wind direction."

and ill prepared for fighting in the rugged terrain of Afghanistan. Like the British army before it, the Soviet army was unable to defend itself against guerrilla fighters who seemed to materialize out of nowhere, ambush tanks or convoys, and then disappear just as suddenly into the caves and hills.

The rebels were not afraid of dying; in fact, the U.S. Central Intelligence Agency (CIA) estimated that the average life span for those Afghan fighters battling Soviet tank divisions was about three weeks. "It's not un-reasonable to assume," notes Junger, "that every Afghan who took up arms against the Soviets fully expected to die."[10]

Total War

The mujahideen attacked communications networks, roads, and bridges. They were willing to allow the Soviet army to control the cities like Kabul and Jalalabad; however, the Soviets had no chance against the resistance

A family in Kabul inspects the damage to their home following a Soviet tank attack. Suspecting civilians of harboring mujahideen rebels, the Soviets deliberately targeted homes, schools, and mosques.

in the countryside. Many villagers helped the mujahideen by hiding them, feeding them, or playing the roll of an information network—relaying messages from one resistance group to another.

By fall 1980 the Soviets stopped focusing entirely on the mujahideen and their resistance groups and began targeting the villages themselves. Their goal was to show the villagers that they were in danger because of the mujahideen. If the villages stopped supporting the resistance, the Soviets believed, the mujahideen could be defeated.

And so the bombing began—planes blasted orchards of fruit trees and fields ready to be harvested. Soviet helicopters hovered over herds of sheep and goats while snipers shot them. The Soviets targeted homes, schools, and mosques. Villagers were questioned and tortured in the hopes of gaining information about the whereabouts of the mujahideen. One man in eastern Afghanistan told a reporter that the home he and his wife had built was bombed. "They are trying to drive us all to [refugee camps] in Pakistan," he explained, "so no one is left to feed the [mujahideen]."[11]

Brutality

In some areas, Soviet patrols tried a different tactic—attempting to establish a friendly relationship with villagers who might betray the mujahideen for a price. In one instance, Soviet soldiers befriended a group of villagers in southwest Afghanistan. After being invited to a village home for a meal, the soldiers believed they might be successful in their mission.

As the food was being served, explains one Soviet intelligence officer, the Afghans attacked. Instead of bargaining with the men, he says, the soldiers learned the depth of the anger felt by many Afghans: "The local guys took our men's guns away, and brought them to the yard and beat them and cut their faces, ears, hands, and legs, and then they cut them into pieces and put them into pots of boiling water. The next day our soldiers went there and destroyed the village, but they never found the murderers."[12]

There was no question that the war between the mujahideen and the Soviets was tearing apart the lives of most Afghans. Many were forced to evacuate their homes, and with crops and livestock ruined, there was little to eat in an already poor country. Even so, many civilians were determined that the Soviets should not be permitted to take over their country. One old man, who was blind in one eye, summed up the feelings of many Afghans: "As long as I can still see out of the other eye, I will fight and kill Russians."[13]

Fighting with American Weapons

As the war dragged on, the United States got involved—secretly. During this time, the Soviet Union and the United States were involved in the power struggle known as the Cold War, a fifty-year period in which both superpowers backed various regional military conflicts but did not openly go to war against each other. Although President Ronald Reagan had no interest in sending American soldiers to fight the Soviets, he found the war in Afghanistan an opportunity to weaken the Soviet Union by helping the resistance.

In 1982 the United States began covert shipments of military supplies to the mujahideen. Billions of dollars in weapons were secretly funneled to Afghanistan by U.S. intelligence agencies. Across the border in Pakistan, the CIA ran camps for Afghan fighters, teaching them how to use the American-made Stinger surface-to-air missiles.

It was the Stingers, say experts, that changed the war. They were easy to use and, weighing only thirty pounds each, were extremely light. And for the damage they did to Soviet aircraft, the Stingers, which cost $75,000 apiece, were a comparatively inexpensive weapon. "In two out of three times that they were fired in Afghanistan," notes one observer, "a Stinger destroyed a Soviet jet or helicopter that cost about $4 million each."[14]

In addition to the influx of weapons into Afghanistan, there was a surge of foreigners anxious to join the jihad, or holy war. By 1986 more than thirty-five thousand outsiders had joined the mujahideen to fight the Soviets. Many came from Arab nations such as Syria and Saudi Arabia, but some fighters came from Malaysia and Pakistan. Approximately sixty nations were represented among these foreign warriors, who believed it was their sacred duty as Muslims to save Afghanistan.

"You Want Many . . . Casualties to Be Small Children"

With its aircraft being destroyed on a regular basis, the Soviet army was the center of controversy at home. The Soviet people were calling for an end to the war, which was costing not only billions of dollars but also thousands of Russian lives. However, the Soviet government was not willing to withdraw from Afghanistan.

The Soviets retaliated, using helicopters to drop millions of mines throughout Afghanistan's countryside. For the mujahideen, the most hated were the butterfly mines, which were colored green and gray and looked enticingly like presents. Soldiers were not the only ones affected by the mines, however. Civilians—especially children—

"What Can I Do?"

In 1985 Debra Denker of *National Geographic* visited Afghanistan in the midst of its war with the Soviet Union. In her article "Along Afghanistan's War-Torn Frontier," Denker tells about her introduction to a young pregnant Afghan woman.

"I will never know this woman's name. Among Afghan villagers it is the custom for women not to tell their names to strangers. On this cold November night she is busily preparing food for the six [mujahideen], Afghan freedom fighters, who have escorted me across the Pakistani border to Afghanistan's embattled Paktia Province and into this small village in the Jaji region.

But in the darkness and snows of December, sometime around the fifth anniversary of the Soviet invasion of Afghanistan, she will give birth to her tenth child. If the child comes in the safety of the night, it will be born here, in this earthen house warmed by an iron stove. If her baby comes in the day, she is likely to be in the damp bomb shelter hewn into the ground under the fields outside the village, her birth pangs accompanied, perhaps, by the roar of jets and bombs.

She pauses to pour me a glass of steaming black tea. 'When the planes come, I can't run very fast to the bomb shelter any more.' she says. 'I am too big and heavy. What can I do?'"

were frequent victims of the butterfly mines, as they mistook them for ballpoint pens or watches, and lost a hand or an eye.

One Scottish doctor at a Red Cross hospital in Afghanistan explained the reasoning behind such mines, which rarely killed a victim outright:

> Most of the mines they've laid are designed to maim, not kill, because a dead body causes no inconvenience. It only removes the one dead person from the field. But somebody who is wounded and in pain requires the full-time assistance of several people all down the line who could otherwise be fighting. And if you want to depopulate an area, then you want many of the casualties to be small children. The most stubborn peasants will give up and flee when their children are mutilated.[15]

"A Bleeding Wound"

Many people did flee—most taking their families to refugee camps in neighboring Pakistan. But the mujahideen stayed, continuing to batter the Soviets, who were becoming weary of the war. In 1987 Soviet president Mikhail Gorbachev acknowledged that the war was "a bleeding wound,"[16] and in 1989, after ten years of war, he ordered the Soviet army to leave Afghanistan.

The price of the war was high, especially in terms of lives lost. Whereas the mujahideen had killed or wounded fifty thousand Soviet

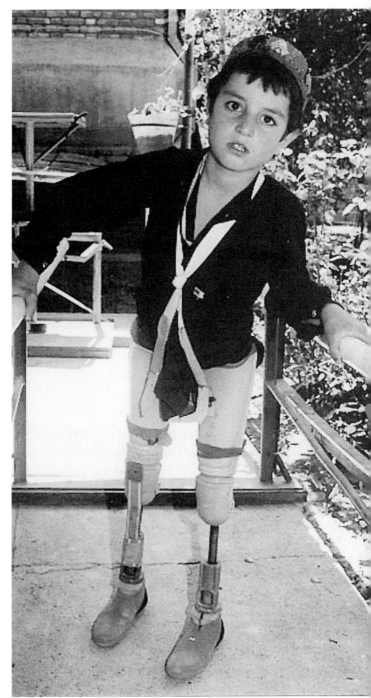

This boy lost his legs to a Soviet butterfly mine, a type of explosive whose appearance was designed to entice children.

Memories of Kabul

In her book *My Forbidden Face: Growing Up Under the Taliban*, a young woman named Latifa recalls the hardships faced in her hometown of Kabul in the final days of the war with the Soviets.

"I recall in particular the winter of 1988–1989. The Soviets were about to leave the country. Kabul was in the grip of the coldest temperatures in living memory. Food supplies were almost exhausted. The [mujahideen] had surrounded and blockaded the capital, and we were running out of everything. My sister and I would line up separately in front of two different bakeries to buy six loaves of bread. It was the same with gas, because the electric towers had been destroyed by the resistance, so everyone was using gas rings for cooking and coal for heat.

Lines were growing longer all over the city. It took half a day to get the least little item. Some people started waiting in midafternoon and reached the head of the line at around seven o'clock; others arrived at the stores well before dawn, sometimes at three in the morning, in the hope of getting their turn at nine. These hardships lasted for four months, and people actually dropped dead standing in line. . . . The Soviet planes resupplying the city landed only at night, and the newspapers spoke of 'Kabul on life support.' With the rocket fire, the endless lines, the price of rice, sugar, and flour, people in the city were nervous wrecks: the slightest thing would set them off and start them fighting among themselves."

troops, more than 1 million Afghan people had died in the fighting. In addition, one-third of the remaining population had fled the country. Though the mujahideen had successfully driven off the invaders, there was little celebrating at the war's end because Afghanistan lay in ruins. The one bright spot, people believed, was that the worst was behind them. It would not be long until they realized how wrong they were.

The Coming of the Taliban

When Soviet troops pulled out of Afghanistan in 1989, they left a land that was in distress. Millions of land mines lay strewn across the countryside, and fields and pastures were mined. Almost every road that had been paved was obliterated, and 5 million Afghan people had fled their homeland to escape the violence.

Civil War

Many of the Afghan people hoped that the jihad was over; after all, they reasoned, the mujahideen had driven the invaders out. Those families who had been relocated in refugee camps across the border in Pakistan wanted to return home. Even though there was a great deal of work to be done to rebuild farms and villages, people were anxious to return.

But it soon became clear that the violence had not stopped. The mujahideen, unable to agree on who should be in charge of the country now that the Soviets had left, turned on one another. Negotiating a new government pleasing to all factions seemed an impossible task. One observer notes, "The same fierce tribalism that had defeated the Soviets . . . made it extremely hard for the various [mujahideen] to get along."[17]

Thanks to the U.S. government, which had furnished more than $3 billion worth of weapons and military assistance over the ten-year war with the Soviets, the mujahideen were heavily armed. Now, however, instead of fighting a U.S. enemy, they were using their missiles and machine guns to kill one another—as well as tens of thousands of civilians caught in the crossfire.

Not Political

Although a great many political differences existed between the factions, many of the mujahideen leaders—often called "warlords"—were fighting for purely economic gain. In the southern provinces, individual warlords fought to establish control over key routes between Afghanistan and Pakistan. Trucks from Pakistan laden with packages of food, tools, or other consumer items from international relief agencies were seized by the mujahideen and sold on the black market.

The mujahideen also set up checkpoints along routes between villages and charged travelers toll taxes. If travelers did not have enough money to pass the checkpoint, they were beaten and sometimes killed. Two journalists from the *London Times* told checkpoint guards that they were United Nations (UN) relief workers to avoid paying tolls, but the local mujahideen were not impressed. On a road in the north between Kundūz and Emam Saheb, the two journalists were ordered to turn their car over to the mujahideen, who needed to pick up supplies from a village some distance away. The journalists learned that travelers had the best chance of a safe trip in the morning. After about two in the afternoon, there is little traffic, they were told, and bandits knew that they would not be caught robbing or attacking travelers then. One civilian explained that another good time to travel was immediately after a checkpoint guard was replaced. "Guards at checkpoints get greedier and greedier," he says. "When too many complaints come in, the [mujahideen] commander moves them elsewhere, and the new ones are a bit more modest in their demands for a while."[18]

Even by taking precautions, most travelers were aware that they needed a great deal of money to satisfy the demands of the warlords. By 1993 many roads had multiple checkpoints within just a few miles of one another—each mujahideen trying to get as much money as possible. "It had gotten so bad in Kandahar [in the south]," says one UN official, "that there were ten different checkpoints requiring ten different payoffs between the airport and the city. It was unlivable."[19]

A group of Mujahideen rebels prepares to lay siege to Kabul during the civil war. After the Soviets withdrew from Afghanistan in 1989, the mujahideen began fighting among themselves for political control.

Afghan farmers harvest opium from poppies. The mujahideen forced many Afghan farmers to grow poppies, the source of opium and heroin, instead of food.

Cash Crops and Satellite Dishes

The warlords also used farmers to make money for them by changing the crops they grew. Although the country was experiencing massive starvation after the Soviet war, the mujahideen knew there was far more money to be made in cultivating the poppy, which is the source of opium and heroin. Farmers trying to reestablish orchards or nut groves were told to tear out such crops and plant poppies instead. Those who refused were killed and their homes set on fire.

The mujahideen sent their soldiers into the fields to help harvest the poppies, and they were smuggled across the border into Pakistan to be processed into heroin. By 1994 Afghanistan had become the world's leading source of opium and heroin, supplying 70 percent of the world's supply.

The farmers themselves saw very little of the profits, but the warlords controlling poppy production lived like kings. One of the mujahideen established his own little kingdom from opium production and smuggling. With a villa that contained crystal chandeliers, a large swimming pool, and a satellite dish that pulled in Western television programming, he seemed unconcerned that less than a mile from his home farmers forced to grow poppies were starving to death.

"What Government?"

The lawless chaos of Afghanistan's countryside extended to the cities, too. The capital city, Kabul, had suffered little damage during the ten-year Soviet occupation. However, in less than four years of civil war, from 1989 to 1993, most of its homes were reduced to rubble. Few windows survived the constant bombardment of rockets, grenades, and Stingers; in government buildings, workers used rocks to hold down stacks of papers so they would not blow away.

One traveler to Kabul during this time observed that the city's zoo was unfortunately in the front lines in the fighting between the mujahideen factions and had fared no better than the city's buildings:

> The white bear is smarting from three bullet wounds, the vulture is limping after a mortar exploded near its cage and shrapnel hit its leg. The deer and the antelopes have been eaten a long time ago. Rumor has it that during one of the numerous battles . . . one soldier mistook the elephant for a tank and tore it to shreds with a grenade.[20]

Lawlessness—a very real sense that no one was in charge—became the mood of the capital city. Garbage piled up in the streets,

and telephone lines and lights that had been destroyed by the bombardment were not replaced. One soldier, asked if the government planned on fixing the ventilation system in a nearby tunnel, shrugged, "What government?"[21]

There was distrust between people; no one could be sure who was, in fact, part of a different faction. For that reason, people were reluctant to buy food from the bazaars, or outdoor markets. The government claimed to have proof that boys belonging to one of the factions had been injecting poison into watermelons and cucumbers.

"I Think We Have Returned to Tribal Warfare"

People—especially women and children— were constantly at risk from the mujahideen fighting in Kabul. Notes one visitor to Kabul, "Women were being raped in broad daylight, and robberies had become as common as shopping."[22] Women from the international relief agencies in the city distributing medicines and food were fair game, too. They were stripped, raped, tortured, and dragged out onto the street by the mujahideen. One citizen was furious with the state of her city. "We have suffered a brutal and savage civil war in this country," she said. "I think we have returned to tribal warfare."[23]

The brutality was unbelievably extensive, including patients in Kabul's hospitals. Journalist Radek Sikorski talked with several female patients who said that rapes and beatings were common occurrences. "It is worse at night when soldiers come with guns and take away the young girls to rape them," said one woman. "I threw stones at them while they did it and told them that it's as if they were doing it to their mother or sister, but they wouldn't listen." She advised Sikorski, "You should put them in jail and shoot them."[24]

Sixteen-year-old Meher said that she had been beaten and raped many times, but she was not sure what to do about it. If she told anyone, she was frightened that she could be punished in a worse way. "My father comes every few days," she said, "but I am afraid to tell him anything."[25]

"I Had a Dream"

This violent, chaotic atmosphere continued throughout Afghanistan until 1994. It was then that it seemed things might change—at least in the southern provinces. A group of Islamic students started to challenge the mujahideen and had some success.

The leader of the Taliban was a local Muslim cleric named Mohammad Omar. Although details of the Taliban's origins are

Led by a Muslim cleric named Mohammad Omar, Taliban fighters like these set out to wrest control of Afghanistan from the corrupt mujahideen in 1994.

vague, Omar has explained that he became angry after hearing about a particularly violent, distasteful crime committed in 1994 by two of the mujahideen. The men had kidnapped and raped two teenage girls from a village in southern Afghanistan and were holding the girls prisoner in their camp.

Omar went to some local seminaries, called madrassas, and rounded up about fifty young men who were students there. Omar led them to the mujahideen camp, where the students freed the girls and avenged the crime by hanging the two men. Two months later Omar and the students went out again—this time to rescue a young boy whom two mujahideen were threatening to rape. Again, they freed the boy and killed the mujahideen during a gun battle in the streets of Kandahar,

Buoyed by their success in fighting some of the mujahideen in the southern part of Afghanistan, Omar and the students—who now called themselves *Taliban*, meaning "students" or "seekers"—set out to take back the country from the corrupt mujahideen. Omar said later that he had had a vision that he and his followers would undertake a holy mission for Afghanistan. "I had a dream," he said. "I dreamed that the Holy Prophet [Muhammad] appeared before me and said we must bring peace."[26]

Who Are the Taliban?

The young students Omar led were mostly Afghans, but the madrassas in which they had been studying were across the border in Pakistan. During the war with the Soviets, millions of people from Afghanistan had fled from their homes. Many in the south—mostly Pashtuns—had traveled to Pakistan, where refugee camps had been established along the border.

In a Madrassa

In his article "The Making of Afghanistan" for the *New York Review of Books*, Pankaj Mishra describes one of the Pakistani madrassas that produced many of the Taliban soldiers trained in the severe ideology of fundamentalist Islam.

"Although it is the biggest of the Pakistani [madrassas] near the border with Afghanistan and quite famous, the [madrassa] had, when I visited it in April [2001], the somewhat lowering appearance of a poorly financed college in an Indian small town: peeling paint, dust-clogged stairs, broken chairs, unfinished buildings bristling with rusting iron girders, and shabbily clad students.

In one corner of the compound was a separate hostel for boys between the ages of eight and twelve—a courtyard lined with curious fresh faces under elegant white caps—who read nothing but the Koran, which they were expected to memorize. In one tiny room at the hostel for older students, many of whom were from Afghanistan, Uzbekistan, and Tajikistan, there was the unexpectedly moving sight of six young men sleeping on tattered sheets on the floor, their turbans respectfully arranged in a row next to the door.

The kitchen consisted of two dingy rooms, their wall stained black from the open wood fires; almost an equal number of flies hovered over the stagnant yellow curry in exposed drains and the freshly chopped mutton on a wide wooden table. . . . But food and lodging were free. And the orphans and sons of poor Pashtuns in the refugee camp . . . wouldn't have had many options."

Near the larger camps, fundamentalist madrassas had also been set up—teaching a form of Islam that was much more conservative than that practiced by most Afghans. The madrassas were open to the sons of the Afghan refugees. Even though the schools had a far more fundamental Islamic view than that of most of the families, parents were glad that their children had somewhere to study. The free room and board offered by the madrassas made the decision of whether to send their sons away an easy one.

The curriculum at the madrassas was fairly limited—most of the day was spent memorizing the Koran, the holy book of Islam. Because teachers at these madrassas believed that the Koran was all a student needed to know, the boys did not learn math, literature, science, or history. Some madrassas offered training in military arts so that the students might someday be capable of defending their religion against nonbelievers. But memorizing the verses of the Koran was the number-one priority.

One British television crew visited a madrassa in 1997 and was shocked to find some of the new, younger students chained to their desks as they recited the Koran. "What was even more appalling," notes one observer, "was that the head of that particular institution defended this practice by saying that the chained [students] would otherwise run away."[27]

Little Resistance

Though the methods of the madrassas were severe and strict, the fundamentalist view of Islam that the students learned made them eager to wage jihad against people who did not have the same views. They were pleased to obey the orders Omar gave them, and soon word of this group of young men and their confrontations with the powerful mujahideen had spread in southern Afghanistan.

Several villages requested the help of the Taliban in restoring order, too. Sometime in early 1995 Omar began to envision the Taliban as more than a police force against the mujahideen. He announced a new jihad against anyone—Muslim or non-Muslim—who was responsible for the suffering of the people of Afghanistan, and he claimed that his job as leader of the Taliban was to direct "the implementation of Islamic order"[28] throughout the country.

As they set out to bring their interpretation of Islamic order to the nation, the Taliban encountered little resistance. Omar accomplished this by sending advance men to village leaders, informing them that the Taliban was on its way, and hoped to get the support of the people. "The Taliban program was simple but astonishingly effective," say political experts Ralph H. Magnus and Eden Naby. "They promised to end the fighting and to restore law and order under the *shari'a* [Islamic law]."[29]

Support for the Taliban

Such promises were welcome to the villagers, who had not seen peace in fourteen years, as well as to traders who were tired of being robbed or forced at gunpoint on the roads to pay tolls to the mujahideen. Many of the mujahideen in those areas, realizing they could no longer bully the villagers, simply moved on. Some mujahideen might have preferred to fight the Taliban but were unsure of the support of their men. "The nightmare of any officer," said one fighter, "is that he must order his men to fire on a bunch of mullahs [Muslim officials trained in religious law] leading a mob. Would they obey?"[30]

A truck carrying Taliban soldiers and weapons stops to allow a herd of sheep to pass along the road to Kabul. Once the Taliban took control of Kabul in 1996, most Afghans felt optimistic about their future.

In less than a year, the Taliban had created a solid base of support in the south and southwest regions of Afghanistan. Thousands of other students from madrassas in Afghanistan and Pakistan joined the campaign. The Taliban also had begun attracting financial support. The governments of Pakistan and Saudi Arabia, both of which hoped to stabilize Afghanistan politically, provided funds for the Taliban. So, too, did Osama bin Laden, a wealthy Saudi who had come to Afghanistan to fight with the mujahideen against the Soviets during the 1980s. Bin Laden agreed with the notion of an ongoing jihad against those who threatened Muslims and offered the Taliban $3 million in cash to purchase more weapons.

"I'd Have Been Glad if Even a Dog Came to Power"

By September 1996 the Taliban had moved north to Kabul. Since 1994, when they executed the mujahideen for their crimes in southern Afghanistan, the Taliban had almost always been able to take control of a region without much violence. Omar's forces took Kabul easily, too. However, they wanted to make sure the residents of Kabul understood the seriousness of their jihad.

The current president and his advisers—set up by several of the mujahideen as a temporary government—had fled Kabul as the Taliban approached the city. Though the Taliban soldiers did not harm civilians, they stormed the UN compound where former president Mohammad Najibullah had taken refuge. Najibullah, a Communist, had been president during the war with the Soviets.

He would serve as an example of how the Taliban would treat their enemies. After beating him, they tied him to a Jeep and dragged him around the city. The following day, his body was hanging from a traffic light. As one young woman who witnessed the spectacle recalls, "The Taliban hung him up for display in the Ariana square with a noose made of steel, the wire cutting into his bloated flesh. His brother suffered the same fate. The Taliban stuffed banknotes into the mouths and noses of the hanged men and attached more notes to their toes, as a symbol of humiliation."[31]

Many citizens were surprised by the violence of Najibullah's death. However, he had been an unpopular president, and many of the residents of the capital remained optimistic about the Taliban. Their city was in ruins from the warring mujahideen, and the Taliban were promising peace. In the beginning at least, most were willing to overlook the execution and support the Taliban. Said one Kabul businessman, "I'd have been glad if even a dog came to power if he brought peace."[32]

"They Came and They Destroyed Everything"

But whereas the Taliban had shown restraint in their takeovers of the cities and villages throughout central and southern Afghanistan, they underwent a dramatic change as they moved north. Northern Afghanistan is populated by a number of non-Pashtun ethnic minorities, many of whom were suspicious of the Taliban members, who were primarily Pashtuns.

"All the People Lost Their Hopes"

Though the Taliban claimed to offer protection from the violent crime that had become common when the mujahideen competed for power in Afghanistan, the Taliban committed a great deal of violence on ethnic minorities who resisted the regime. The following is an excerpt from an interview included in Rosemarie Skaine's *The Women of Afghanistan Under the Taliban*.

"When the Taliban came into our village, they burned the green garden and destroyed cultivated land because they said the force of Ahmed Shah Massoud [a man who fought against the Taliban] had buried ammunitions in the gardens and lands and they wanted to set them off. It was really a bad time. You could see that your whole village was burning. Our village was very famous for its grapes and berries and the economy of the whole people depended on the exporting of fruits. As their gardens were turned into ashes, the whole village migrated to other places. Some went to the northern provinces and some to the west, but most of them went to Kabul and from there those who had money went to Pakistan.

Our village that was once the most beautiful and rich in fruit . . . in the whole region now has turned into a desert and it is very difficult to rebuild it. All the people lost their hopes and even some decided to get the citizenship of other countries and never return to Afghanistan."

The Taliban destroyed this boy's house and those of many others in northern Afghanistan. There, the Taliban ruthlessly subdued non-Pashtun ethnic minorities, people whom they viewed as inferior.

North of Kabul, in the villages of the Shomali plain, the Taliban no longer sent advance teams to encourage cooperation. Instead, they used missiles and bombs to pound residents into submission. One old man explained that because of the Taliban, he had lost everyone he loved. "My wife is dead," he cried, "my son is dead, my four daughters are dead. Only I am left, no one else."[33]

The Hazaras, an Asian-looking people who are the descendants of Mongol invaders from the thirteenth century, were especially targeted. The Taliban stormed into Hazaran villages and went from house to house, rounding up all men and boys and shooting them. "They came and they destroyed everything," sobbed one man who fled his village, "shooting and killing people—even donkeys—with knives and poking the eyes out of the people with steel rods. They did not leave a single house standing in my village."[34] Another Hazaran mother of six says that she was forced to watch her husband burn to death at the hands of the Taliban. "They locked him in our hut and set fire to it, then held me there listening to his screams," she says. "They killed 300 people in my village, even children and old men and burnt all the crops."[35]

The Massacre at Mazar-e Sharif

Nowhere else did the Taliban show more violence toward civilians, however, than at Mazar-e Sharif, a northern city that had been the site of battles between Taliban and resistance fighters for more than a year. In 1998, nine months after being driven back, the Taliban returned.

Years later, the massacre at Mazar-e Sharif would be known as the worst civilian atrocity in Afghanistan's history. Several thousand people died, many of them children as young as five or six. Witnesses described the Taliban's actions as "a killing frenzy" against "anything that moved."[36] Specifically, Taliban troops systematically searched for men and boys among the Hazaras. Thousands of them were marched to the city jail and then transported to other cities—presumably for execution.

According to the international organization Human Rights Watch, the men and boys were loaded into large container tracks capable of holding between 100 and 150 people. In at least two known cases, when the trucks reached their destination, almost all of the prisoners had died of heat stroke or asphyxiation inside the closed containers. Altogether, the number of Hazaras killed at Mazar-e Sharif was more than 2,000.

One man, who survived the mass execution when a fellow prisoner fell on top of him, says that the Taliban's jihad had nothing to do with waging war against enemies of Islam. Instead, he is certain that the Pashtun Taliban were guilty of ethnic cleansing—killing off cultures and ethnic groups that were different from their own. "It was clear that Mullah Omar ordered the Taliban to . . . kill all the people," he says. "He once made an infamous statement: that all the Tajiks should go to Tajikistan, the Uzbeks to Uzbekistan, and the Hazara to Ghoristan."[37] (*Ghoristan* is the word for "cemetery.")

"By God's Grace"

The Taliban did not try to keep their massacre a secret. In fact, they erected a large sign at the site of the killings. "By God's grace," it says, "the Taliban captured the northern region of Afghanistan in 1998, and massacred the pagans."[38]

And although many Afghan people lost their lives during the Taliban's campaign to

One of the most controversial actions by Taliban leader Mohammad Omar took place early in 1996 in the city of Kandahar. In his article "Stoners" for the *New Republic*, reporter Andrew Meier describes the occasion that left many Afghans—including an important part of the anti-Taliban resistance—talking about Omar and the Taliban.

"In Kandahar's mosques the mullahs gather long before dawn each day, led by Mohammed Omar, the one-eyed head mullah. Earlier this year, Omar called together the Taliban's ruling council to witness a great drama. Omar, who is all of 35, unlocked the holiest shrine inside the central mosque, cloaked himself in the purported shroud of [the prophet Muhammad], fell to his knees before his awed fellow mullahs and at last emerged in the light to crown himself the 'Amir Muminin,' the 'King of All Muslims.'

The news was too much for the folks in Kabul. 'How can anyone dare call himself the Amir?' asks Ahmed Shah Massoud, who controls Kabul and the northeastern provinces. . . . As he takes tea in Astalef, a remote mountain village forty minutes from Kabul, Massoud, who is in his 40s, remains confident and composed despite the Taliban's ceaseless rocketing of Kabul. 'How can anyone believe what he says? To claim to be the Amir is to claim to govern all the Islamic people of the world, the Algerians, the Iranians, the Saudis—these people do not look lightly at such a claim.'"

control the country, many survivors consider the deceased the lucky ones. Within hours of their conquest of a village or a city, the Taliban set out to establish a new set of laws and a new system of justice. The people of Afghanistan, who had lived through almost two decades of war, soon found that life could get much, much worse.

3 Life Under the Sharia

To emphasize the change in government, in 1996 the Taliban changed the name of the country to the Islamic Emirate of Afghanistan. The nation would be governed by mullahs and religious scholars rather than politicians. And the new government would be, noted Taliban officials proudly, the only one of its kind anywhere on the planet.

"These Principles Are Eternal"

Mullah Mohammad Omar was the supreme head of the government. His edicts were automatically law—there was no legislature to vote on policies. Omar did preside over a ten-member council, called the Supreme Shura, which he could consult on particular issues facing the nation.

Of course, thousands of Taliban were needed to make the new government work—from regional and local governors and judges to soldiers, police, and checkpoint officers. Roughly thirty-five thousand Taliban—most from Afghanistan but many from Pakistan and other Muslim nations—were responsible for running the country.

The guiding principle was called the sharia—an old-time, rigid form of Islamic law. In the hands of Mullah Omar and his Supreme Shura, the already rigid system of law became even more unforgiving. The Taliban allowed no compromises and no adaptations to modern life. Since some of the features of the modern

world (especially Western influences) were seen by Omar as the cause of the nation's problems, change was unthinkable. As one Taliban leader explained in 1996, "There is no possibility of change in Islamic principles, which have not changed in the last 1,400 years. These principles are eternal, and they will remain eternal."[39]

The Rules

Soon after Taliban soldiers marched into a village or city, they made it very clear that everyone was expected to follow new rules. There was to be no television or music. Prayers were to be said five times each day, without exception. Women were to wear the burka in public and were not permitted to hold jobs or attend school. Men were not allowed to shave their beards.

At first, many Afghans had welcomed the Taliban because they were putting an end to the warring mujahideen. However, when these rules were announced, they were less enthused. "Historically, Afghans are pretty much live and let live about religion and social issues," says one UN Afghanistan specialist. "They really don't have a tradition of allowing anyone to tell them how to live their lives."[40]

But the Taliban aggressively insisted on total compliance with their interpretation of sharia. Lest there be any misunderstanding, a large force of Taliban soldiers and police

Taliban police officers use rods to coerce Kabul residents into a mosque. The Taliban routinely used whips, guns, and other extreme measures to enforce compliance with the sharia, a strict form of Islamic law.

worked hard to enforce each new rule. For instance, when the local mullah called people to prayer, police would force passersby into nearby mosques at gunpoint. To keep people from going about their business in cars during prayer time, steel cables were stretched across roads until prayers were over. Within a month of the Taliban coming to power, one local aid worker announced that Afghanistan's strict, unyielding attitude toward its citizens had made it "the most fundamentalist place on earth."[41]

"They Have No Idea of Islam"

One of the key factors in maintaining the rules dictated by Omar and his council was the Ministry of the Promotion of Virtue and the Prevention of Vice (PVPV). The ministry's title was taken from a passage in the Koran, which urges people to learn to embrace things that are allowed and to reject things that are prohibited. Under the Taliban, however, the list of prohibitions was very long. In fact, to many people of Afghanistan, the laws enforced by the PVPV seemed frivolous and arbitrary.

One twenty-seven-year-old Afghan man argues that the mullahs created laws that they claimed were based on the Koran's teachings. Yet when one reads the Koran, he says, such laws are not mentioned at all. "Although they call themselves mullahs," he says, "they have no idea of Islam. Nowhere does [the Koran] say men must have beards."[42]

Yet PVPV squads were unyielding in their enforcement. A man was not only required to have a beard, but he also had to have one at least as long as a fist. If not, he was likely given a few lashes with a whip and jailed until his beard had grown. One Kabul man had a skin disease that made it difficult for him to grow a beard. After being stopped by police in the marketplace, he tried to explain why his beard was not the required length. The police officers only laughed at him, and he spent the next five months in jail.

The Dangers of Music

Some of the most arbitrary laws created by the Taliban prohibited music, dance, and other aspects of Afghan culture. Listening to music was illegal, and one visitor to Afghanistan discovered the seriousness of the ban. Riding toward Kabul in a cab, his driver nervously stopped several miles outside the city to change the cassette tapes of pop music to which they had been listening to one of chants of Koran verses. Had he not done that, the driver told him, they would have been beaten by the guards at the checkpoint.

One shopkeeper in Kandahar verified that even first offenses of listening to music could be brutal. "Last week a man was caught listening to music," he recalled. "The Taliban police beat him badly, tied him up, hung his tape recorder around his neck and paraded him around town in a jeep to show us what would happen to those who did not follow the law."[43] In Kandahar, police at a city checkpoint confiscated so many music cassettes that they strewed what seemed like miles of the shiny brown tape on city lamp poles.

The ban on listening to music was hard on many Afghan people, but it took a particularly high toll on the stores that used to sell music. In Kabul two brothers who used to sell about one hundred cassettes per day said that business during the time of the Taliban could not have been worse.

The shelves that once held rock, folk, and other music from Pakistan, India, and Afghanistan were almost empty. The only permitted tapes were tuneless religious chants by the Taliban—tapes that had been sold to the brothers by armed soldiers. Among other titles were "Taliban Arrived and Ruled," "We're Happy Now and Have Forgotten All the Difficult Times," and "Taliban, O Taliban, You're Creating Facilities, You're Defeating Enemies." Shah Mohamad, one of the brothers, was disgusted at the way the Taliban were able to dictate what people could listen to. "I hate this society," he said. "Everyone does."[44]

"I Can't Live Like This"

Not only were people forbidden to listen to music, but the Taliban also decreed that both singing and playing an instrument were illegal as well. Whenever the PVPV squads did their random checks in homes for weapons, they smashed any musical instruments they found. As a result of the ban, within a few months of the Taliban takeover many of the nation's best musicians had either fled the country or were begging on street corners for money, food, or firewood.

Distraught Afghans could not believe that their love of music could possibly be against the teachings of the Koran. Some citizens found that life without music was intolerable and were willing to risk the wrath of the PVPV. One musician began practicing vocal exercises in his home with a heavy blanket draped over his head. He admitted that he was afraid, but he explained, "I'm without my music. I can't live like this."[45] Those who were caught, however, paid a price for singing. When the PVPV discovered a group of young men singing at a Kabul wedding, they jailed the twenty-one-year-old bridegroom. "We sang very quietly," he remembers, "but the police came inside and beat us."[46]

Taliban officials explained the ban by insisting that music was anti-Islam. They claimed that there was a little-known record that Muhammad once warned people not to listen to music, "lest molten lead be poured into their ears on judgement day."[47] One Afghan man maintained that the Taliban made mistakes in their interpretation of the Koran simply because they were not edu-

Police arrest a group of men caught playing cards, one of the many social activities the Taliban perceived as anti-Islamic.

Art, Taliban Style

One of the rules that the Taliban enforced was the banning of any artwork or photography that showed the faces of living things. In his article "A Last Road Trip Through Pre-modern Afghanistan," relief worker John Sifton describes some hotel artwork after it had been "corrected" by the Taliban—and his own reaction to it.

"The bathroom in our room didn't work, so we had to go down two floors to use another one. On the landing of the stairs two floors down, there was a large landscape painting, about 16 feet by 12 feet, of a pond, some flowers, a forest and a few animals. The heads of the three animals had been cut out of the painting to comply with Taliban aesthetic restrictions: the creation of images of living beings is forbidden under the Tal-

iban's kooky interpretation of Islamic law. This left a decapitated deer standing by a pond and a headless beaver sitting on a tree stump.

I considered the piece as I stood on the landing. A terrible painting . . . done entirely with two shades of green and one shade of brown and then vandalized by Taliban police trying to ensure its innocence before God without destroying it altogether. In its own way, I thought, it is a post-postmodern masterpiece. But surely I could add still more to this artwork. I could buy it from the Taliban, sell it for a fortune in New York, and give the money to the Taliban opposition. . . . I was still chuckling to myself when one of the Afghan engineers came down the stairs. 'What are you laughing at?' he asked. 'I don't know,' I answered."

cated. Although the students had indeed memorized Koranic verses, he says, most of them were unable to read and write. "These are no educated people in this administration," he says. "They are all totally backward and illiterate."[48]

At the office of the Artists' and Musicians' Central Union in Kabul, the president of the association not only agreed with the idea that the Taliban were backward, but he also was counting on it. The office's entire collection of musical instruments was hurriedly hidden to avoid being destroyed, except a grand piano that was covered with a sheet. The association's president explained that the piano was too big to hide, but he felt that the PVPV might not even know that it was a musical instrument. He said, "They probably will think it's a table."[49]

"They Can Go to the Parks and See the Flowers"

In addition to banning music, the Taliban government outlawed many other forms of entertainment. Television and radio, condemned as tools of corrupt Western societies, were prohibited. Movie theaters were closed permanently. Museums, including the National Museum in Kabul, were closed and more than 70 percent of the priceless art pieces were looted.

Kite flying and raising pigeons—two favorite pastimes in Afghanistan—were banned because they were thought to distract people from studying the Koran. Sports such as soccer were acceptable, as long as the players did not wear shorts since the Taliban considered shorts on men to be extremely lewd. The

Members of the Taliban burn reels of film outside a Kabul theater. The Taliban banned all movies, music, and other forms of popular media that they believed subverted the teachings of the Koran.

spectators at such matches had rules, too. They were not permitted to clap or cheer for the players and only could say "Allah-o-akbar," which means "God is great." And it was not only Afghans who were required to adhere to the rules; when an unsuspecting Pakistani team came to Kabul in 1997 to play a match, their players were arrested for coming onto the field in shorts.

One girl says that she was most saddened by the ban on celebrating the Afghan new year, called Nowroze, which she and her family had always thought to be the most exciting time of the year. The official pronouncement stated that "these frivolous activities are relics of a pagan time, before the coming of the Prophet [Muhammad]. They are not fit for

Muslims, only for infidels. Anyone celebrating *Nowroze* will be whipped."[50]

By removing culture and entertainment from Afghanistan, noted one Afghan scholar, the Taliban cut the heart out of the people. "Any chance the Taliban get," he said, "they take away any Afghan-ness—their ways, their customs, their uniqueness. . . . What they are trying to do is tell the Afghans that they have no cultural identity."[51] A teen living in Kandahar put it more succinctly: "We're like dead people."[52]

One Taliban official did understand that fun could not be entirely removed from Afghan life, although his definition differed from that of many people. "Of course, we realize that people need some entertainment," he said, "but they can go to the parks and see the flowers, and from this they will learn about Islam."[53]

Love Under the Taliban

The arrival of the Taliban also meant dramatic changes in the relationship of the sexes. No longer was it permissible for a boy and a girl to date—or even be seen together. Marriages were to be arranged by parents, and any friendly or romantic relationship between a young woman and a young man was forbidden until the two were married.

There were many ways that the PVPV could discover such relationships. Most of the time they cruised the streets in their pickup trucks, stopping hurriedly if they saw a young couple. If the two were not married or re-lated, they were both arrested. Another way was listening in on private telephone conversations. If a PVPV officer heard a couple talking about dating or meeting, he traced the telephone number back to an address and made his arrests.

For some young Afghans, the ban on dating was a challenge to overcome. Many never really considered obeying that law, and they found ways to get around it. In a society where so much was forbidden, they were willing to risk a beating or jail time for the fun of dating. Some set up secret meetings by using younger brothers or sisters as messengers. Others used codes so that an eavesdropper would not realize they were discussing a date. One young man says that he and his girlfriend invented matching stories for PVPV squads in case they were stopped. "I was afraid," he admits, "but I proved to the Taliban that [Nuria] was my sister."[54]

"The New Year Felt Hollow and Empty"

One of the most enjoyable times of the year for most Afghan people was the celebrating of New Year's Day, or Nowroze. The day centered around family picnics, games, and music. However, as an Afghan woman named Hala recalls in Yasgur's book *Behind the Burqa: Our Life in Afghanistan and How We Escaped to Freedom*, the Taliban was quick to outlaw that holiday.

"This had always been one of my favorite days of the year when I was growing up. When people could, they journeyed to Mazar-i-Sharif to picnic. . . . A special flag, called a janda, was raised. If the flag ascended the pole and started to fly without difficulty, people congratulated one another and said that it would be a good year. . . .

Our celebrations took place at the home of the oldest, most esteemed family member. It was traditional to wear new clothing, to symbolize the start of a new year. All kinds of traditional foods were served. Each food symbolized good luck, sweetness, or new beginnings. . . . *Nowroze* was also a time for games. Men participated in playing *buz kashi*—a traditional game played on horseback. Young girls were encouraged to walk barefoot on green grass. There was music and laughter. There was a sense of family and a wonderful feeling that the world could be renewed again and again.

The Taliban outlawed all new year's practices, from raising the flag to games. . . . We continued to observe as many traditions as we could in the privacy of our homes, but we were afraid. . . . For the first time, the New Year felt hollow and empty."

But for those young people who did not break the law, the result was often loneliness and depression. At Kabul Mental Hospital, doctors say that about 40 percent of the patients they have treated during the Taliban's rule suffered from depression related to heartbreak. "Love is a necessity," says one doctor. "It's not just oxygen and water that keep people alive."[55]

Amputation as Punishment

Beatings and imprisonment by the Taliban's police were common punishments for what the government considered minor offenses— kite flying, listening to music, and so on. However, for serious crimes, the Taliban enforced punishments that were unspeakably brutal, including the amputation of hands, feet, or both.

Taliban officials execute a woman accused of adultery in full view of a capacity crowd at a Kabul soccer stadium. The Taliban often staged brutal public punishments and executions to serve as warnings to others.

"The World Is Upside Down"

In her book *My Forbidden Face: Growing Up Under the Taliban: A Young Woman's Story*, Latifa describes the numbing depression that overtook families as the rules of the Taliban put an end to their routine lives.

"Everything has changed; the world is upside down. My father still rises early for his morning prayers, but can no longer go jogging because the Taliban will not allow anyone besides themselves to run in the street. Soraya, Daud, and I still get up around nine or ten o'clock, without any energy, without any enthusiasm. My father and brother are obliged to grow beards, and we all feel our faces drooping from sadness and fatigue. No one turns on the radio now because there is no more news, no more music, no more poetry. Nothing but propaganda.

And decrees:

'It is forbidden to whistle and to own whistling teakettles.

It is forbidden to keep dogs or birds.'

I was right. Luckily our canary is already long gone. We, and no one else, granted him his liberty. But now we must part with Bingo, our white greyhound, whose fur is so dense he looks like a bear cub. He has always been part of my life."

Fourteen-year-old Muhammad Daoud, who was a marketplace worker during the year the Taliban took over Kandahar, was accused of stealing money. He was taken to jail and beaten by police. The teenager never appeared in court, but after two weeks in jail he was sentenced by a mullah whom he had never met. The punishment, he learned, was to have his right hand amputated as crowds of people watched. After putting a tourniquet on his arm one of the Taliban gave him a local anesthetic to numb his arm, and another man began cutting his hand off with a surgical knife. "He cut through the skin," recalls Daoud, "and I saw bood, and then I passed out."[56]

As was the case in most other public amputations, the hand was held up by the thumb for all to see. Afterward, Daoud was taken to a hospital, where he remained for three weeks while doctors tried to repair the botched amputation. Daoud lost only a hand, but many other accused thieves faced amputation of both hands or of a hand and a foot—depending on the amount of money stolen.

How Best to Kill

According to their interpretation of ancient sharia, Taliban judges (usually mullahs) would order perpetrators of more serious crimes, such as murder, to be killed in the way they killed their victims. Hence, a man who killed someone with a gun would be shot by his victim's brother. One who killed with a knife had his throat slit.

One Taliban official explained that homosexuals needed to be executed in a very severe manner, but he found himself torn between two possible ways. "Some say we should take these sinners to a high roof and throw them down, while others say we should dig a hole beside a wall, bury them, then push the wall down on them."[57] Witnesses say that the second choice was widely used, with "men

Taliban deputies crush cans and bottles of beer with a tank. In keeping with the teachings of the Koran, the Taliban expressly prohibited the consumption of alcohol.

caught in homosexual acts . . . propped up against any convenient old wall, which was then toppled onto them by a tank."[58]

Couples found guilty of adultery were punished by stoning. According to the Taliban's interpretation of the sharia, the stones used must not be any larger than the palm of one's hand, lest those sentenced die too quickly. Unlike other public punishments under the Taliban, spectators were often encouraged to take part in stoning.

"It Was a Good Thing"

One such stoning took place in Kandahar in the summer of 1996. The Taliban had learned that a woman and a man had engaged in a sex-ual relationship without marriage, and the government wanted to make an example of the couple. On a hot afternoon in late August, with temperatures topping one hundred degrees, people were summoned to the front courtyard of a large mosque, where the execution was to occur.

The condemned couple was brought to the site on the flatbed of a truck as approximately six thousand people crowded around. Taliban officials made space for the relatives of the accused, including small children. The woman, Nurbibi, was buried in a pit so that only her head and shoulders were above ground. The man, Turyalai, was made to stand blindfolded in front of a stone wall.

There were two separate piles of stones, and according to custom, the Taliban judge threw the first stones at each of the accused. After he was through, Taliban police and soldiers threw a flurry of rocks, killing Turyalai in about ten minutes. It took longer for Nurbibi to die, and the Taliban officers invited spectators to throw rocks to speed the process.

Executions such as this one brought about mixed emotions from the Afghan people. One teacher in the crowd thought that the stoning was a positive experience. "It was a good thing," he said. "The only way to end this kind of sinning."[59] However, some of the younger spectators said that they did not like the Taliban-run executions and amputations. "I was very scared," said one ten-year-old boy. "I don't like these things, and I couldn't watch."[60]

Screams to Frighten Crows from Their Nests

As word spread throughout the nation of the government's quick, violent punishment of criminals, the Afghan people grew more and more afraid of the PVPV squads that roamed the streets of the cities and towns. In many cases, the PVPV squads seemed to be a law unto themselves—police could arrest and punish citizens without a trial or order from the region's mullahs.

One man who had been part of one of the PVPV squads says that his commander not only allowed his officers to beat citizens but also encouraged it. According to this officer, his commander told his men that it was important for them to become "so notorious for bad things that when you come into an area, people will tremble in their sandals. Anyone can do beatings and starve people. I want your unit to find new ways of torture so terrible that the screams will frighten even crows from their nests and if the person survives he will never again have a night's sleep."[61]

People became so terrorized that they tried to ingratiate themselves with the Taliban by turning in their neighbors for crimes. "As we drove around at night with our guns," he says, "local people would come to us and say there's someone watching a video in this house or some men playing cards in that house."[62]

Although many Afghan people bemoaned the Taliban's effect on society, government officials were pleased. One Taliban deputy noted that the new justice system was so successful that he predicted the Taliban's message would be admired and copied by nations everywhere. "Since we have lit the torch of truth in Afghanistan," he said, "naturally it will light the torch in other countries."[63]

CHAPTER 4

Women Under the Taliban

Although all Afghan people were placed under severe new restrictions by the Taliban government, no group endured stricter rules than women and girls. So harsh were these restrictions, in fact, that the Physicians for Human Rights, an organization that monitors the treatment of citizens, noted in 1998 that they were unprecedented. "We are not aware of any place in the world in recent history," stated executive director Leonard Rubenstein, "where women have so systematically been deprived of every opportunity to survive in the society—from working to getting an education, to walking on the street, to getting health care."[64]

Women Before the Taliban

As is true in many nations, Afghanistan has a history of repressing women, especially in the southern Pashtun areas where the culture is conservative. In these regions, men have always been the decision makers who have total control of their households.

Yet in the years before the Taliban—even during the years when the Soviets controlled the government—women had been making great legal strides in Afghanistan. In 1984, for example, the Afghan Labor Law guaranteed equal job opportunities for women. As a result of that law and continuing educational opportunities, more and more women were working outside the home. In Kabul women made up more than 70 percent of teachers, 40

percent of doctors, and more than half of all university students. By 1995 Afghan women were serving in such diverse jobs as pilots, deans of universities, army officers, engineers, and judges.

"Women Just Aren't as Smart as Men"

When the Taliban regime seized power, however, one of its first decrees was to limit what women could do. No longer could they hold a job or go to school. In fact, they were encouraged to remain in their homes, raising children and doing housework. If they did leave the house, they had to be accompanied by a male relative.

Taliban officials had varying explanations for such dramatic changes. One regional governor gave his understanding of why women should not hold jobs. "Women just aren't as smart as men," he confided. "They don't have the intelligence."[65] Other officials maintained that the new restrictions were not so much an indictment of women's abilities but rather a show of the Taliban's respect for women. During the civil war, when the mujahideen were kidnapping and raping young women, no one rose to defend the victims until Mohammad Omar. By keeping women indoors—or else in the company of a male relative who could defend them—the Taliban insisted that they were protecting the women of Afghanistan according to the sharia and the laws of Islam.

The Burka

Nothing symbolized the loss of women's freedom under the Taliban more than the burka. Outside the home, women were required at all times to wear the long, heavy bag that covered them from head to toe, with only a two-inch-by-two-inch mesh opening in front of the eyes.

Burkas had been worn by a small segment of the population before the Taliban, but most women in the cities had never even seen one prior to the Taliban's rise to power. On the contrary, many women in the cities were used to wearing contemporary clothing, getting ideas for clothes from American or European women's magazines. "I'd never owned a [burka] in my life," says one Kabul woman. "Most women in Kabul had never even worn a scarf over their heads."[66]

Taliban officials insisted that the burka was protection, keeping women safe from the prying eyes of men. "Women need protecting," he said. "[Burkas] keep order. This tradition means women are cherished, unlike the West, where they are treated as rotten pieces of meat by men who just throw them away. If a woman wears a [burka] she respects God." Besides, he added, "there are pretty [burkas]. Women love wearing them as part of their identity."[67]

Mullah Omar agreed, but he maintained that the protection works both ways since the sight of a woman had dangerous effects on Muslim men. Said Omar, "A woman's face corrupts men." He explained that women who "are going outside with fashionable, ornamental, tight and charming clothes . . . should never expect to go to heaven."[68] To remind women that the burka law was for their own protection, cities such as Kabul were flooded with large posters proclaiming, "A woman covered is like a precious pearl in an oyster."[69]

"This Dirty Life I Have"

When the Taliban decreed that women were not allowed to work, the government ensured that millions of women and children would be forced to live in poverty. In this excerpt from an interview in Rosemarie Skaine's *The Women of Afghanistan Under the Taliban*, a young mother explains how prostitution was the only way she could support her children.

"A few months later, my younger child became sick. I took him to hospital but the doctor diagnosed her [with] kidney problems and must be operated on. I had no money to buy the items and medicine for the operation. I asked the manager of the hospital to make the medicine free for me, but he told me that the hospital itself does not have any pharmacy. I sat all day at the front gate . . . and begged everyone to give money for my child. One day a handsome Pakistani gentleman came. . . . I went with him; he was living alone in his house. Suddenly he gave me 1,000 rupees from his pocket and asked me to let him do anything with me. . . . I knew there was no other way and my child would die. . . . I know it is an immoral thing, but there is no other way out. Though I am young, I am ill and I can't do begging all the day. My children are too small to work. I don't care about the Taliban, I have no honor in society. I am alive just for my children. . . . When they become young adults, I don't want to be alive even for a minute. Death is much better than this dirty life I have."

A Kabul woman wears a burka covering her entire body, while her daughter is permitted to show her face. Taliban law required women over the age of ten to keep every inch of skin hidden from public view.

"My Face Belongs to Me"

Although Omar and the other Taliban officials said that their edicts were based on the teachings of the prophet Muhammad in the Koran, many people were skeptical and countered that the Taliban had made up such rules. "The Taliban are doing more than interpreting Islam," said one UN diplomat. "They are restructuring Islam."[70]

Nancy Hatch Dupree, an expert on Afghanistan's history and society, says that laws such as the one demanding that women wear the burka are based not on religion but rather on conservative social customs. "The Taliban are reinforcing the patriarchal norms," she writes, "wrapped in the mantle of Islam."[71]

One young Afghan woman was furious at the notion that the Koran demanded that women's faces and bodies be covered. After trying on a burka for the first time, she felt angry and humiliated. "My face belongs to me," she writes. "And the Koran says that a woman may be veiled, but should remain recognizable. The Taliban are trying to steal my face from me, to steal the faces of all women. It's outrageous!"[72]

"I Was Invisible"

Many Afghan women vehemently denied that they liked wearing the garment at all. They said that a burka was hot, smelly, and could make the wearer claustrophobic and dizzy. One woman said that she had trouble wearing her burka while riding in a car because the heat and smell of the material nauseated her. Another woman recalls that dust from the street swirled up under her burka and stuck to her lips. "I felt like I was suffocating in stale air," she says. "It also felt like I was invisible. No one could see me, no one knew whether I was smiling or crying. The mesh opening didn't give me enough view to see where I was going. It was like wearing horse blinders."[73]

A London journalist visited Kabul in March 2001 to experience what life under the burka was like for Afghan women. She was appalled at the concentration it took just to remain upright:

> As I walked through the crowded marketplace, head down and feet shuffling, I was only dimly aware of the woman scuttling beside me through the stifling heat of the blue [burka]. . . . Instead, I concentrated on maintaining the correct subservient distance from my male chaperone a few paces in front. It was a difficult task because the crocheted panel that covered my eyes prevented me from really seeing where I was going, and I was in constant danger of being run over by cars in the street.[74]

Painted Windows, Plastic Shoes

Once in their homes, Afghan women were allowed to remove the burka. However, the Taliban also required that windows facing the street either had to be painted black, or else have curtains closed so that no man could see a woman from outside without her burka. Cars, too, had to have darkened windows or screens on all but the windshield, lest a female passenger be seen without the burka.

In the months that followed the Taliban's takeover, there were other restrictions on clothing, too. Shoes such as high heels were banned because the noise was arousing to some men. As an alternative, many women wore shoes of cheap (but quiet) plastic. White socks, too, were banned. Unsure of the reason for the ban, Afghan citizens surmised that it was because white was the color of the Taliban flag, but government officials denied the claim. The socks themselves were provocative, they decreed, and should never be worn.

The punishments for clothing crimes usually involved a beating. PVPV squads roamed the streets armed with lengths of steel cable and would hit women for showing skin, hair, or wearing the wrong shoes. One Afghan woman, a doctor, recalls how—in the days after the Taliban came to Kabul—she was frequently in such a rush to get to the hospital that she was not completely covered. "[The Taliban police] would hit us and spit on us," she says, "and then we would have to come in to the hospital and do our work."[75]

Sometimes the punishments were life threatening. One newspaper reported that a woman caught without her burka received a public beating of one hundred lashes with a whip. Asked if she had seen the account, one Afghan woman reacted with pride in the way the victim took her punishment. "Oh yes," she said. "We know of this. She fainted after sixty lashes, but she never cried out."[76]

Lots of Orders to Fill

The burka became such a necessity that Afghan clothing makers were working overtime to meet the demand. "It's steady work," smiled one burka seller at a bazaar. "I have a lot of orders to fill."[77] Another seller admitted that although business was good, he felt a bit guilty selling a garment he knew was unnecessary. "According to Islam," he said, "a woman's face and hands can be uncovered, so the Taliban's order is not Islamic. I can make more money from what the Taliban have done. But I don't agree with it."[78]

Many women were angry to find that the garment—which they did not want to begin with—was very expensive. Prices in Kabul ranged from the equivalent of five dollars (a little more than the average Afghan's monthly salary) to ten dollars for a burka with a finer texture. Many women were too poor to buy one and were doomed to being prisoners in their homes. In some villages, women desperate to have a little time out of doors pooled their money for a single burka and took turns wearing it.

Girls whose families had been killed in the civil war were particularly victimized by the high price of burkas. Since the Taliban decreed that any girl over the age of ten must wear one when outside, girls at the state-run orphanages all had to remain inside because none owned a burka. In one Kabul orphanage, every girl aged ten and older actually stayed indoors for the entire five-year period the Taliban was in power—from 1996 to 2001—although boys went outside every day.

"I Cry Seeing the Classrooms Locked"

Even if girls and women wore their burkas, the Taliban would not allow them to attend school—whether elementary, high school, or university. The reason, said government officials, was that Afghanistan did not have the money or facilities to have two separate school systems, one for girls and one for boys. And because separation of the sexes was crucial to the Taliban, they insisted that the boys needed education far more than the girls, who only needed to raise children and stay home.

As a result, many schools that were formerly girls' schools were closed. One such facility was Malali High School, a girls' school in Kabul. All through the years of civil war, the school had been pounded by mortars and rockets, its walls crumbling and windows cracked or missing.

Even so, the school's five hundred pupils attended faithfully, studying science, history, literature, and languages until October 1996, when the Taliban ordered it closed. "I cry seeing the classrooms locked," the school's caretaker admitted. "A mullah accompanied by several armed Taliban came and demanded the keys. They told me the school would be turned into a [madrassa]."[79]

"I Damn the Taliban"

Without the routine of classes and school projects, the limited lives of Afghan girls became numbingly boring. Most girls stayed indoors, helping their mothers tend to younger children. Older girls, many of whom were partway to a college degree when their studies were cut short, felt cheated out of the possibility of an interesting career. "I was a second year student at Kabul Medical Institute," one young woman said angrily, "but a long time ago the doors of knowledge were closed. This is a big disaster. I don't know about my future. Where can I go? I damn the Taliban and fundamentalists."[80] Another girl confided that since the Taliban's ban on education closed her school, her lessons

"Edict Number One"

In her book *Veiled Threat: The Hidden Power of the Women of Afghanistan*, Sally Armstrong includes several edicts that the Taliban announced as soon as they gained control of Kabul. The following is Edict Number One, which details several new rules—many of them concerning women. The translation was done verbatim by staff at the United Nations.

"1. No exit and traveling of sisters without escort of legal close relatives.
2. Those sisters coming out of their homes with legal escort should use veil [burka] or similar things to cover the face.
3. Sitting of sisters in the front seat of cart and Jeep without legal relative is forbidden. In the case of appearance, serious measures will be carried out against the vehicle and cart driver.
4. Shop keepers do not have the right to buy or sell things with those women without covered face, otherwise the shop keeper is guilty and has no right to complain.
5. Cars are strictly forbidden to be covered with flowers for wedding ceremony and also are not allowed to drive around the city.
6. Women's invitations in hotels and wedding party in hotels are forbidden.
7. Sisters without legal close relative with them cannot use taxis, otherwise the taxi driver is responsible.

8. The person who is in charge of collecting fares (money) for sisters in buses, mini-buses, and Jeeps should be under ten years old."

The Taliban prohibited women from sitting in the front seat of cars and carts.

were a distant memory. "I used to know how to read," she said, "but I've forgotten everything."[81]

Ironically, the ban on education for girls and women affected the education of boys. Since the vast majority of teachers were women, many boys' schools had to close their doors, too. In January 2000 a UN agency found that in Taliban-controlled areas (about 80 percent of the country) a record-high 75 percent of boys were not attending school. Noted one sociologist, "A whole generation of Afghans is growing up without any education."[82]

Men Have to Work and Defend God

Whereas the ban on education damaged the minds and spirits of women under the Taliban, the lack of health care damaged them physically. In a country already lagging behind developing nations in health care, the new government's rules, which made it difficult for sick women to be treated at hospitals and clinics, were debilitating.

One Taliban official explained that, ideally, every citizen would receive medical treatment. Just as with education, however, separate facilities were absolutely necessary for men and women, and the new government did not yet have the resources to provide care for both. As a result, the Taliban established priorities. "We cannot provide for everybody," he said. "Men need to be strong to work and defend God, so they are the priority."[83]

The biggest obstacles to Afghan women receiving health care were Taliban rules. For example, female patients could only be seen by female doctors. Even little girls could not be examined by a male doctor. However, there were not enough women doctors to treat the large numbers of Afghan women requiring care. Many doctors—male and female—had been among the millions of educated people who fled Afghanistan during the civil war and the coming of the Taliban. In addition, the Taliban's rules against women holding jobs outside the home diminished the staffs at city clinics and hospitals. Even when the govern-

Women sit outside an Afghan health clinic waiting for treatment. Afghan women in need of medical attention faced long lines, substandard facilities, and a shortage of doctors.

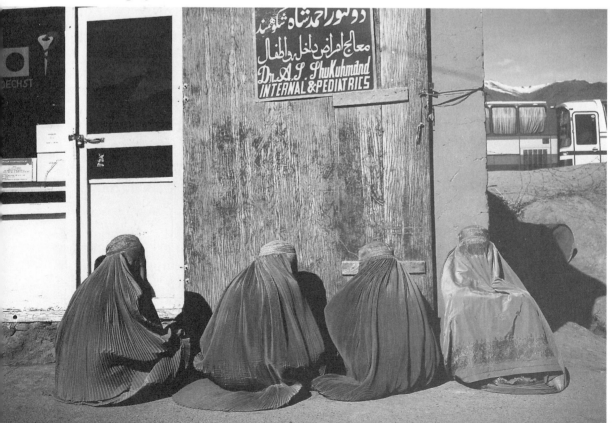

ment relaxed the rule and allowed some female doctors to return to work, the ban on women's education cut the number of medical students almost in half.

"The Wards Were Primitive and Filthy"

Women could not be treated in the same wards as men and were frequently relegated to basements or outbuildings so that they did not come in contact with men. One visitor to a women's ward in Kabul was horrified at the unsanitary conditions endured by the female patients: "The wards were primitive and filthy. The bathrooms were indescribable and there was excrement everywhere. There were empty beds and dirty mattresses and hardly any medical staff. The patients didn't get food unless their family brought it for them, and there was very little medicine."[84]

In another section of the city, a reporter saw seriously ill women being sent to "a crumbling old building that has no windowpanes, no running water, no proper operating room and barely enough electricity to power light-bulbs."[85] It is not surprising that many of the patients seen there for even relatively minor health problems died from infections.

Endangering Doctors and Patients

Though the Taliban relaxed the rules about female doctors being able to work, many of these doctors reported that they were frequently abused on their way to and from work by PVPV squads. "One day the religious police may stop me on the street and ask where I am going," one Kabul health worker said. "At that point, the fact that I have 'permis-sion' may mean nothing to him; he can beat me or harass me or arrest me at his whim. Every day I leave my house and I pray that I might get back home safely at the end of the day."[86]

Even inside the hospital, Taliban guards made it difficult for the staff to work. Doctors and nurses—even in women's wards—were required by law to wear burkas, although most medical personnel removed them when there were no PVPV police around. But the police dropped in at all hours and seemed to take delight in punishing medical workers not covered by a burka. "Two nurses told me how they were beaten with a tree-branch for not wearing [burkas]," says one reporter. "When one of the women tried to run away, the guard forced her to the ground and held her between his legs while he beat her with the stick."[87]

In addition to abusing health care workers, Taliban police were also a threat to the patients themselves. In one hospital, PVPV squads ordered all female patients—even those close to death—to go home. The reason, they explained, was that because the ward was so crowded, the Taliban guards could not guarantee that their modesty and virtue would be preserved.

Though many male doctors say that they did not agree with the Taliban's policies, the menacing presence of PVPV police frightened them into refusing help to female patients. One woman says that her baby daughter was suffering from severe diarrhea and dehydration. No facility existed for female patients nearby, so she and her husband took the child to a male-only hospital, which would not treat her. As a result, the child died within a few hours. "With her body in my arms, we left the hospital," says the woman. "It was curfew time, and we had a long way to get home. We had to spend the night inside a destroyed house among the rubble. In the morning, we took my dead baby home."[88]

A World of Troubles

As a result of such policies, the state of women's health in Afghanistan deteriorated during the years of the Taliban. By 2000 the life expectancy of a woman was about forty-one years. One in twelve died during childbirth—the second highest rate in the world.

Afghan doctors say that the women they treated suffered from sexually transmitted diseases (STDs) at an appalling rate—25 percent of their female patients over the age of thirteen tested positive for STDs, even though these women were by law homebound. This was an especially dangerous state of affairs in a society in which a woman could

be given the death penalty for being unchaste. As one doctor explains, "They get [the STDs] from their husbands."[89]

The toll on women's health was so overwhelming that it is almost impossible to measure, say experts. Dental care was nonexistent for women since dentists were not allowed to remove the burka's veil to examine an infected tooth. Widows could not go to the doctor because they did not have a male relative to accompany them outside. The list goes on and on.

Depression, not surprisingly, was by most accounts epidemic among women under the Taliban. Being treated as nonentities was disheartening for millions of Afghan women. One Kabul woman said that she felt nothing but despair and sadness:

It's been six months since the Taliban arrived, and I don't want to leave my house.

The Eradication of Afghan Women

In her article for *Time* magazine entitled "Tyranny of the Taliban," reporter Christiane Amanpour describes the harshness of the Taliban's treatment of women she witnessed firsthand in Kabul as well as the lengths the government would go to keep it a secret.

"We were standing in Kabul's only hospital for women when the purist authorities of the Taliban decided they did not want any pictures taken. Screaming and shouting at us, they grabbed our TV cameras, all our tapes, and even our briefcases. Several armed Taliban enforcers slapped a cameraman, while another rammed his rifle butt at visiting aid workers. One raised his hand toward Emma Bonino, the European Union Commissioner for Humanitarian Affairs, there to investigate the Taliban's treatment of women, and would

have struck her but for an aide's intervention. The next thing we knew, a truckload of armed men were escorting us to the central police station. After several hours, they freed us and returned our cameras but refused to give back the tapes. 'Now I know,' says Bonino, 'what the people of Kabul have to live with every day.' . . .

From the day they marched into Kabul, the Taliban's adherents have sought to eradicate women from public life. In a land where the women have had to work while the men fought, the regime has barred females from taking any job outside the home or even leaving their houses without a male relative to accompany them. Girls have been thrown out of school. Foreign-aid agencies have been forbidden to offer any of their services or assistance directly to females."

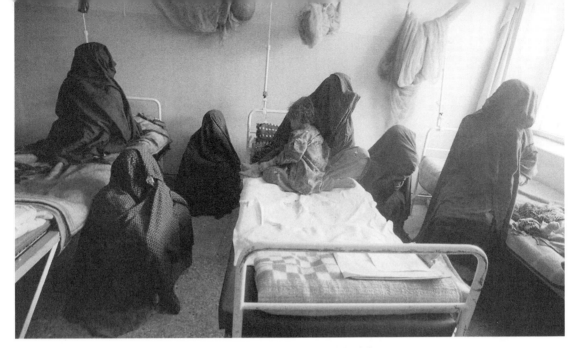

Six women share a hospital room with only three beds in rural Afghanistan. As a result of the poor medical care available to Afghan women, female life expectancy was shortened to just forty-one years.

I start to laugh or cry and I don't know why. I feel sad all the time. And I cannot concentrate. The other day I was helping someone with accounting and I realized I'd entered the same number over and over again. I have no hope for my future, and what's worse, I have no hope for the future of my two children.[90]

"A Woman Is Half of a Man"

Although most experts in Islamic tradition say there are no edicts in the Koran that can account for the Taliban's treatment of women, some Afghan citizens believe the answers can be found in the early lives of Taliban members. "At a very young age they were orphaned or separated from their families," says one Afghan woman. "They did not grow up with their own mothers and sisters, who were lost or who died during the war. They were taken to very strict religious schools. They were controlled and indoctrinated, and never encountered a woman. Their teachers taught them that a woman is half of a man."[91]

UN diplomat Haron Amin agrees that the Taliban turned women into subhumans whose lives were a nightmare. "One of the minsiters of the Taliban said that there are two places for a woman," he recalls. "One is the husband's bed, and the other is the grave-yard. This is an official quote that is the woman's place in the world."[92]

Such pronouncements were not surprising to Afghan's women. One young woman, whose medical studies came to an abrupt halt when the Taliban seized power, was without hope. "Afghan women have no rights today," she shrugged. "They are all walking deads."[93]

5 A Life of Grinding Poverty

The gusto with which the Taliban enforced its fundamentalist interpretation of the sharia was undoubtedly its major strength. What was difficult for Taliban officials was the day-to-day running of a nation that had been devastated by war since 1979. Roads had not been repaired, most of the cities had no electricity or running water, and the buildings that had been destroyed by mortars and bombs had not been cleared away or rebuilt. It was, remarked many citizens, as if the Taliban had no other plan for governing Afghanistan than creating new laws and arresting and beating people who did not obey them.

"Slowly Afghanistan Is Coming to a Halt"

Some citizens were philosophical about the new leaders. "We have religious scholars running our government," said one man. "How can someone educated only in matters of religion run a state?"[94] Others wondered whether the Taliban were really educated at all, since they seemed to hold the educated people of Kabul—the doctors and other professionals—in contempt.

Nessar Rahmad, a Kabul telephone company worker, says that the Taliban official chosen to direct the company knew nothing besides the Islamic teachings he had learned at the madrassa in Pakistan. The man opposed the use of computers because he did not trust the monitors. He had little understanding of the running of a telecommunications office, and he did not seem to want to learn. "The only thing he cared about," remembers Rahmad, "was that we have a long beard, wear a turban, and say the prayers."[95]

Taliban officials were moved frequently from the war front (the Taliban continued to fight against resistance fighters throughout their regime) to bureaucratic jobs and back to the front. As a result, few gained any experience in government jobs. Because female workers had been fired, many offices were completely empty. Those workers who remained did their work surrounded by young Taliban soldiers who did little but lounge on chairs and sofas.

As the nation's infrastructure continued to erode, so did the Afghan people's hope that life under the Taliban might improve. One observer was not hopeful. "Slowly," he wrote, "Afghanistan is coming to a halt."[96]

"People Are Cold All the Time"

The Afghan people could not rely on the services usually provided or overseen by the government—electricity, water, and so on. The Taliban government was without money; almost every dollar it collected in taxes went to purchase guns and ammunition for the fight against the resistance. Little was left over for rebuilding, as was obvious by the shuttered stores and dark factories.

As a result, jobs were scarce in the cities. In Kabul, 70 percent of the people were unemployed. Teachers and government workers who once considered themselves middle class in Kabul were scraping by on less than the equivalent of about five dollars per month. "A monthly salary here is worth less than a pack of Marlboros," said one Red Cross worker, "and nobody can live on that."[97]

Many Afghan people were attempting to survive on far less, however. In a Kabul bazaar, a man selling apples said that even at a penny a pound, few citizens could afford even the brownest, most mushy fruit. The carrots, cauliflower, and other produce at the market were rotting in the stalls, too, for no one had money.

Bread, Tea, and Cold

More than one-third of Kabul's population depended on the international relief agencies that sent in truckloads of food. With a pink ration card, one could stand in line to receive five pieces of flat bread. Many people survived on one meal a day—bread and a little weak tea. Water for the tea was often in demand, however, since curbside spigots were the only water source, and these were turned on only three hours each day.

Hunger was not the only problem faced in the city. The cold, too, was a problem. At night, temperatures frequently dipped below

Many Afghans subsisted on meager rations of bread provided by relief agencies. These boys are fortunate enough to have extra loaves to offer for sale.

Afghanistan's Orphans

There were many orphanages before the Taliban came to power, but they had many female workers. When Kabul fell to the Taliban, this Kabul orphanage, like many others, felt the effects very quickly, as John-Thor Dahlberg writes in his *Los Angeles Times* article "Afghan Orphans Face a Pitiless Future."

"For the children at Daurul Itom, the hardships keep coming. . . . When the Taliban banned women in Kabul from working, the orphanage lost all but four of its 350 female employees, and the 100 men who work there have been poor substitutes at mending and washing clothes, teaching school, or acting as surrogate mothers. 'All the children do now is sleep and eat,' said [interim director Abumoslem] Mokhtar.

Because Kabul's banks have been shut down for most transactions since the Taliban occupied the city, the orphanage cannot buy food. . . . It has been three months since the orphans last tasted meat, a staple in the Afghan diet. Now, they say, they are hungry all the time. . . .

The orphans used to bathe twice a week. But since the women left, they get one bath a week, in warm water carried upstairs in pails. They have no good shoes or socks, no toys, few books. . . . But the one thing they really wanted last week was a ball they could play soccer with in a barren field near abandoned Soviet army field kitchens. Their ball had a puncture.

'I dreamed a few days ago that all my friends came to class, and there were enough balls for everyone,' one young boy said. 'Then I woke up, and it was just another morning.'"

Under the Taliban, orphanages like this one in Kabul lacked adequate food, had no bathing facilities, and provided the children with few sources of entertainment.

freezing, and most buildings and homes had no heat at all. Families that could afford it bought a little coal or wood and huddled around a fire at night. Neither fuel was cheap, and people had to choose whether they would spend money on firewood or bread since they could not afford both. Even a purchase of firewood or coal did not guarantee warmth for an entire night. Said one firewood seller, "People are cold here all the time."[98]

As a result of the cold and rampant malnutrition in Kabul and other cities, health workers said that sickness was common. And because of the constant inhaling of burning wood or coal, doctors were seeing record numbers of patients with severe lung ailments such as bronchitis and pneumonia.

Inventing Jobs and Simply Begging

With such unemployment, poverty, and need, it is not surprising that hundreds of thousands of people in the cities turned to alternative ways of survival. Some women—especially widows—became prostitutes. Banned from working, and with families to feed, women risked the wrath of the PVPV squads to earn a bit of money.

Many people stood on city street corners trying to sell their possessions. Women who were once middle-class workers stood with their business suits and dresses strewn at their feet, hoping someone would buy them for only a fraction of their original cost. One man stood holding a child's bicycle in one hand and a radio in another. "I have to go out on the street," he said disgustedly, "and sell what I own."[99]

Some tried to find inventive ways of making a little money. Old men stood for hours each day in some of the road's worst potholes, hoping that drivers might throw them a few cents in return for the warning. One old man, who had lost his ration card, earned a little bread by offering to stand in the long, slow lines for other people. Children looked for scraps of paper or wood to sell as fuel. A twelve-year-old boy spent five hours each day knocking on doors holding his incense burner. For a penny or two, he would perform a ritual blessing of the home.

Many Afghan people simply begged. Women, afraid to go outside because of the Taliban, would send their children out to beg, even toddlers. One family boasted that with seven children, it had once made fifty cents in a single day. Some beggars stood outside mosques hoping people would feel generous after praying. Others would wait outside restaurants, pouncing on food scraps that kitchen workers poured into the gutters. It was demeaning, and it was often in vain. Said one man, "This is for a dog, to live like this."[100]

A Crisis in Health Care

The lack of an economy under the Taliban affected health care, too—and not only for women. *New York Times* reporter Barry Bearak, who visited Kabul in 1998, found that children's health care was almost nonexistent: "The x-ray machines have no film. The burn unit has been shut for lack of gauze and ointments. When a child needs a shot, parents are sent to the bazaar to buy the medication and a syringe. No records are kept of the 500 youngsters treated each day as outpatients, for this requires stationery and there is a shortage of paper and pens."[101]

The problems were intensified because of a dispute between the Taliban and certain international relief agencies. The agencies, which had been providing medical supplies and help to Afghanistan, objected to the Taliban's treatment of their workers and were promptly expelled by the government. The victims in the dispute, Bearak observed, were children who desperately needed medical help, and now faced a life-threatening situation, such as a baby born prematurely who was in a cracked incubator. "A few rooms away were four new machines ready to be uncrated," Bearak writes, "but no one knew how to use them. The day after the equipment arrived, the relief agency that bought them was expelled by the Taliban. . . . With it went the workers who knew how to operate the incubators."[102]

With little more than fifty dollars per month allotted to hospitals by the Taliban and an antagonistic relationship with agencies that could help Afghanistan, it is little wonder that the nation's health care system was in crisis. In addition to the shortening life span of women, many of whom were denied health care, Afghanistan's children, too, were in trouble. One child in four died before age five—most from illnesses that should not have been life threatening.

Dangerous Customs

Rural areas were especially threatened by the lack of medical care. In the most remote areas, people often tend to follow customs that their ancestors followed—but which are medically dangerous. For example, newborn babies often die of tetanus because many Afghan mothers wrap the cut end of their babies' umbilical cord with potentially germ-ridden muddy leaves until it heals.

Because medical relief workers were not allowed to travel freely in Aghanistan under the Taliban, they could not teach people safer practices. Nor could they offer help with birth control, which a majority of Afghan families wanted. The Taliban banned all forms of birth control, saying that it was the duty of married people to have many children to grow up as soldiers for Islam. The average Afghan woman has seven children in her lifetime—the first born when she is twelve or thirteen years old.

Childbirth was one of the worst health threats in rural areas—to babies as well as mothers. In Purag, a village two hours south of Kabul, there was a small health clinic but no one to staff it. "We try to carry the pregnant women to Kabul," explained one resident, "but by the time they get there, sometimes they or the baby are dead."[103]

Air Soup

In addition to the dangers of childbirth and disease, rural people faced massive food shortages. Severe droughts in key growing areas left many families surviving on little more than grass and wild roots. In one region, 108 children in 378 families died within four months, many of them victims of malnutrition.

Though the Taliban government was certainly not to blame for the droughts that minimized the harvests of wheat and other staples, it was responsible for the lack of irrigation throughout much of central and northern Afghanistan. The underground canals, called *karezes*, were systematically destroyed by Taliban soldiers in their fight to control these regions. Many Afghan farmers say that the *karezes* were sabotaged in an effort to kill off ethnic groups the Taliban considered inferior to themselves.

As a result of natural and man-made problems, food was as scarce in the country as

Women use tablecloths to filter muddy water from a stream. As a result of chronic drought and a lack of irrigation in Afghanistan's rural areas, many villagers grew severely malnourished.

it was in the cities. To try to fool their children into believing they were eating something, many rural mothers served "air soup" to their children—a few particles of flour floating in hot water. The most vulnerable people, the very old and the very young, succumbed to malnutrition, however, often with startling speed. "One morning I went off to town to beg for food," a man said sadly, "and when I came back, two of my children were dead."[104]

"We Want to Stand on Our Two Feet"

Experts in Afghanistan say that besides the physical toll of starvation and sickness, there was a breakdown in the social custom that is central to people in rural Afghanistan—sharing. Since ancient times, Afghan people have believed that one of the most important actions is helping someone else. They also

In his article "A Last Road Trip Through Pre-modern Afghanistan" for the *Peace Pledge Union*, international aid worker John Sifton describes the level of poverty he encountered among refugees fleeing Afghanistan.

"The next day was a nightmare: human suffering on a shocking scale. Displaced persons without enough food to eat were drinking water taken from muddy ponds—mud really. 'They're drinking mud,' I said into my tape recorder. 'They're drinking mud.' I remember one particular experience especially. We were in a windy camp for displaced persons, and a man was showing us the graves of his three children, who had died of disease on three consecutive days: Thursday, Friday, and Saturday. It was Monday, and he had buried his last child the day before. After he described all this, we stood around the graves in the strangely loud silence of the wind, hot as an oven, and the man absent-mindedly adjusted a rock atop one child's grave.

It was a very emotional moment, yet I didn't really feel sad. I was just fascinated by the realness of it all. You look out an office window, and you see a displaced family living in a bombed-out school, sleeping on the balcony and cooking some birds they caught, doves. This is their life. They can't change the channel."

believe that when someone helps them, they are honor bound to return the favor.

"What has enabled Afghans to survive in these harsh conditions," explains one UN relief worker, "is their society of mutuality. If a neighbor does something for you, you have an obligation to repay. Even if you don't [have money] you have an obligation to do something good for someone else who is in need."

But because there are fewer people who have food, a warm home, and other necessities than ever before in Afghanistan, the custom of sharing has virtually eroded. "The number of needy people is so large," says the UN worker, "that the coping mechanisms of sharing are no longer viable."[105]

The erosion of their system of helpfulness both frustrates and angers Afghan people. While they appreciate the foreign aid that has helped feed them, they feel they have lost some self-respect. "What the people of the international community are doing in humanitarian aid," says one Afghan, "we are grateful for that, but we don't want our country to be a begging nation. We want to stand on our two feet."[106]

To the Camps

Though many Afghan people tried to remain in their own cities and villages, millions of others felt safer in refugee camps. Some Afghans had already fled during the civil war, and although they were at first anxious to return to their homes after the war, what they heard about the Taliban made them realize it was dangerous to do so.

Some of the camps were in areas of Afghanistan that had not yet come under the control of the Taliban forces. Some farmers who had at first wanted to remain on their land changed their minds when their wells dried up during the years of drought during the late 1990s. Hearing of camps that offered food and medicine for refugees, many

Afghans loaded up a few belongings and left home.

One farmer heard of a camp near Herat, in western Afghanistan, and decided to move his family there. However, when he arrived, he learned that there was no more food at the camp than there had been at home. Eighty thousand other refugees were there, too, many of them sick and malnourished. In one month, the only food he received for his family was a little rice and a handful of moldy dates. His eight-year-old son, already severely underweight, became ill with pneumonia soon after arriving at the camp, he says. The boy died, largely because there were not enough medicines to treat the hundreds of refugees who needed attention. He held up a plastic strip that once held twelve aspirin and said, "All they gave me for my son was this."[107]

The lack of medicines and supplies for refugees was not limited to the Herat camp. In January 2001 more than four hundred people—most of them babies and young children—froze to death in three different camps. As it was later discovered, the victims had only a few blankets and sheets among them, which were completely inadequate during the icy blizzard.

Many Afghans fled cities and towns and made their way to refugee camps like this one in the Panjshir Valley. Life in the camps, however, was often as bleak as it had been at home.

"This Is What We Eat, Sir!"

John Sifton, a young man working for a relief agency in Afghanistan, was appalled by the number of displaced people he saw there. He found that many Afghan people were both desperately hungry and at the same time ashamed of their inability to fend for themselves. "People eat wild plants, garbage, insects, and old animal parts discarded by butchers," he observed. "In one camp, an old man showed me a bowl filled with rotten cow bowels, grass poking out in places. 'This is what we eat, sir!' he said, wiping away tears with his fist."[108]

Relief workers were saddened by the conditions in Afghanistan's refugee camps. Agencies knew, for example, that the Afghan people needed a minimum of 400 million tons of grain to feed themselves, but in 2000 the country was capable of only producing about 2 million tons. Yet when UN agencies requested aid from their members, the resulting pledges were disappointing. In fact, of the $229 million requested for aid to the Afghan people, the United Nations received pledges of only $18 million.

Ironically, much of the reason for the "donor apathy," as it is often called, was the Taliban government itself. Its growing record of human rights violations, from abuse of women to its excessive physical abuse of criminals, made the international community more eager to impose sanctions, or limits on aid, rather than supply much-needed food and medicines.

Fleeing Afghanistan

Many refugees went to camps outside Afghanistan's borders. One fifteen-year-old

"I Have Lived Too Long"

People who had seen Kabul before the civil war and the takeover of the Taliban were appalled at the change in the city. In his article for the *New York Times* titled "An Afghan Mosaic of Misery," reporter Barry Bearak describes his impressions of the nation's capital in early 2000.

"The suffering is extraordinary.

An estimated 70 percent of the working age population of Kabul is jobless. For men, work is hard to find; for women, it is forbidden. Afghans in the countryside are thought to be better off; they can live off the land. In Kabul, there is nothing to reap from the dead factories or the shuttered stores.

People sell their possessions on the street, their cooking utensils and their picture frames and their extra clothes. Competition is keen, customers few. At dusk, hundreds of women come outside to beg, desperate for a pittance before the 9 P.M. curfew. Dressed in the all-encompassing [burkas], they look ghostly in the aqueous light of oncoming headlights.

Older people recall a worldly Kabul, a city with fine wares and good restaurants and easy laughter. But the memories sometimes startle them, like the tingling in the stump of an amputee. An elderly carpet seller, Haji Abdul Hakim, began to weep and could not stop, thinking of days when he sipped tea with buyers from New York.

'I have lived too long,' he said. 'I shouldn't have lived to see this.'"

girl from Mazar-e Sharif in the north says that her family went south, believing it had a better chance of survival in Pakistan. The family was lucky because it was able to get in one of the better camps—one with one-room mud houses rather than flimsy tents. Even so, the camp was crowded and uncomfortable. "There's nothing beautiful here," she said. "There are high walls around it, and an armed guard at the gate keeps track of who comes and goes. Everyone keeps chickens, and a lot of goats and sheep wander around. There are almost no trees. In the summer, it's like living in an oven."[109]

Still, she insisted, she was not complaining because her family was better off. She was not required to wear a burka in Pakistan, and she was permitted to go to school. Another woman at the camp agreed, saying that just being able to shed her heavy veil was worth it. "Just the feeling of the sun on my face," she smiled, "is a real liberation for me."[110]

Closing the Border

In 2000, however, Pakistan began closing its border with Afghanistan. More than 2.5 million refugees had streamed across the border, and the camps and border towns were overflowing. Even when the borders were shut, thousands camped nearby—waiting. "I am a farmer," said one camper, "but there is no water, no food in my village. I have nothing. I am here for the last four days with my family. All night, all you can hear are children coughing and crying. It is cold. We have nothing."[111]

Refugees waiting at the border had been so desperate that on several occasions when Pakistani officials had opened the border to allow those with passports or visas through, stampedes ensued. In November 2000 thousands pushed toward gates; many people were trampled, and a small child was killed.

In Debt to People Smugglers

Some refugees used professional people smugglers to help them escape the Taliban in Afghanistan. Charging about fifty dollars a head, smugglers guaranteed their customers safe passage to either Iran or Pakistan, past Taliban patrols or border guards. In many cases, however, the refugees did not have the full amount for the smugglers once they crossed the border.

The Barati family, two parents and eight children, found themselves in this situation. They were smuggled out of Afghanistan into Mashhad, a city in the eastern part of Iran where four hundred thousand other Afghan refugees had settled. Mrs. Barati and her two daughters, aged ten and eleven, were working each day in their tiny hut shelling pistachios. They were trying to raise enough money to pay rent as well as to repay the smugglers. "Every day we start shelling the pistachios at five in the morning," she says, "and go on until nine at night. We usually shell six kilos between us."[112] From the pistachios, she and her daughters were making about two dollars per week—not enough to pay the smugglers after paying the rent. Mrs. Barati was frightened because the smugglers had been coming around demanding their money and threatening to kidnap her husband if they did not receive payment.

Another refugee learned firsthand how serious the smugglers' threats were. Her two oldest sons, ages eleven and twelve, were seized by smugglers to whom she still owed money. "They are keeping them hostage in a house in Zabol [near the Afghan border]," she said. "All I have is a telephone number, which

A boy harvests opium poppies. Although Taliban officials publicly condemned opium cultivation, in truth the government derived substantial tax revenue from poppy farmers.

I'm to call when I get hold of the money. But where am I going to find almost $100?"[113]

Opium

More and more Afghan people left the country, and most of those who stayed were living in poverty, trying to survive on one scant meal a day. One group of Afghans, however, was making plenty of money—poppy farmers. This was a surprise to many people in and out of Afghanistan; the Taliban had criticized the mujahideen for its insistence that farmers grow the flowers that yielded opium.

When they first came to power, Taliban officials had promised the international community that farmers would no longer be able to grow poppies. In 1996 one official stressed that "growing a crop that will produce an illicit drug is evil and against Islamic law, just like using an illicit drug. This is written in the Koran."[114] But while the Taliban claimed they were stamping out opium production, the truth was that they were encouraging farmers to grow more poppies. Fighting against the resistance was expensive, and it was impossible to tax Afghan citizens who were unemployed and starving. But by levying a very high tax on poppy farmers and opium producers, the Taliban government was able to make a great deal of money.

"I Know That Opium Is a Bad Thing"

By 1997 more and more farmers were being pressured to change their crop to poppies. It was an easy change because the drought had been bad for the wheat growers. Poppies need very little water, and soon farmers throughout the country were producing more poppies than ever. Some admitted that they had mixed feelings about growing something that was used to make drugs. "Opium is our only gold," said one. "For many years, it has been very difficult feeding my family. I know that opium is a bad thing, but through selling it I now have money to feed and clothe my family, and I have also been able to rebuild our house, which was destroyed by the [mujahideen] several years ago."[115]

The increase in opium from Afghanistan drew international criticism, especially from countries with rising rates of opium and heroin use. Tony Blair, Britain's prime minister, angrily denounced the Taliban for profiting from drugs that find their way to cities throughout the world. "We know that the Taliban regime is largely funded by the drug trade," he said, "and that 90 percent of the heroin on British streets originates in Afghanistan."[116]

The Taliban did not deny the effect of Afghanistan's opium on illegal drug sales in other nations. In fact, one mullah acknowledged that it was because heroin was used by foreigners that the Taliban supported its production. "[Growing] opium is permissible," he explained, "because it is consumed by *kafirs* [non-Islamic people] in the West and not by Muslims or Afghans."[117]

Such statements—as well as the continuing human rights concerns—only served to increase the friction between the Taliban government and the outside world. As the international community worried about the increasing drug trade and the abject poverty in Afghanistan, however, it was unaware that the Afghan people were involved in another export even more dangerous than drugs.

A Training Ground for Terrorism

The Taliban's fundamentalist interpretation of the Koran dictated more than guidelines for criminal justice and the lack of freedoms for women. It also urged Muslims to defend their religion at any cost against non-Muslims. It was, the Taliban insisted, the highest honor for a Muslim to die fighting against infidels, or nonbelievers. In fact, the Taliban looked to a future global war in which Aghans and other Muslims from all over the world could join together and defeat the enemies of Islam.

The Taliban regime had more immediate matters to attend to when it first came to power in Afghanistan, however. The money it made from the opium trade was used to fight against those mujahideen armies that resisted it, especially in the north. However, by the end of 1996 the Taliban had found another source of income—one that gradually made the idea of an Islamic worldwide struggle a real possibility. The source of income was a person rather than a commodity—and his name was Osama bin Laden.

Osama bin Laden

In 1996 Bin Laden was a wealthy forty-one-year-old Saudi with the same radical Islamic views as the Taliban. Bin Laden's father had been a construction contractor, and his connections within the Saudi government enabled him to be given projects such as refurbishing important shrines in Mecca.

When the man died, his estate was worth more than $5 billion—and $80 million went to his son Osama.

Eager to help in Afghanistan's war against the Soviet Union, the twenty-three-year-old Bin Laden had used his own money to finance the recruitment, transportation, and arming of thousands of Arabs who were anxious to join the fight against the Soviets, too. He brought in bulldozers and dump trucks and Saudi engineers as well so that the Afghans could build roads, ammunitions silos, and trenches along the front lines.

Although many of the mujahideen were grateful for the support of Bin Laden and his Arab supporters, others were suspicious of their fundamentalist view of Islam. "My jihad faction did not have good relations with the Arab-Afghans during the years of jihad," said one Afghan fighter after the Soviets left Afghanistan. "We will ask them [the Arabs] to leave our country. Bin Laden does more harm than good."[118]

Al Qaeda Comes to Afghanistan

Bin Laden returned to Saudi Arabia after Afghanistan defeated the Soviet army. However, when the Saudi government allowed U.S. troops to be based in the country after Iraq's invasion of Kuwait, Bin Laden was outraged. Saudi Arabia is a holy place to Muslims, especially cities such as Mecca and Medina. To see U.S. soldiers and their families—non-Muslims—walking around on the streets of these cities was shocking, and Bin Laden said so.

He repeatedly urged the Saudi royal family to send the Americans home, but he was rebuffed. In fact, he was so vocal about his hatred for Americans and his criticism of the Saudi royal family that his citizenship was revoked. He moved to Sudan, where he established a loose network of militant Muslims who were as eager as he was to drive the United States from Saudi Arabian soil. This network was called al Qaeda, which means "the Base."

Al Qaeda, Bin Laden hoped, would cause so much trouble to the United States that it would be forced to withdraw from Saudi Arabia—and all other Muslim nations. The growing knowledge of Bin Laden's al Qaeda activities made Sudan's government nervous, however, and it quickly evicted him.

"A Good Fit"

In 1996 Bin Laden returned to Afghanistan. He quickly established dozen of al Qaeda camps throughout Afghanistan as well as in other countries in the Middle East, including Egypt, Somalia, and Sudan. These were not the simple military camps for soldiers, that Bin Laden had helped to create during the 1980s; instead, they were training facilities for Islamic terrorists.

The Taliban had no qualms about bin Laden's terrorist activities. In fact, notes one expert, "Osama bin Laden was a good fit for the Taliban."[119] The Taliban regime was equally funadmentalist and was eager to fight the infidels of the West. Rather than keep his terrorist activities secret from the government, as he had been forced to do in Saudi Arabia and Sudan, bin Laden could count on

In 1996 Osama bin Laden established al Qaeda training camps in Afghanistan with the full support of the Taliban.

A Loud Welcome

As writer John Miller found in 1999, Osama bin Laden was a celebrity in Afghanistan for his acts of terrorism against the West. In his article "Greetings, America. My Name Is Osama bin Laden" for *Esquire* magazine, Miller describes the tumultuous welcome Bin Laden received when his motorcade arrived in the country.

"The gunfire started with a few shots, but in seconds it was thundering. On cue, dozens of Arab men began firing their rifles into the air when the headlights of the first four-wheel-drive vehicle crested the mountaintop. . . .

Just before this explosive welcome, I had been told, 'Mr. bin Laden will be here shortly.' The tall bearded man with the elaborate turban had not introduced himself by name, but he seemed to be, for lack of a better title, Osama bin Laden's press secretary. 'We have prepared a great welcome. Whenever he comes, there is always a celebration.'

Yellow trails from tracer bullets streaked at odd angles, crisscrossing the black, starcrowded skies. Fireworks shot up, and sparks fell like orange rain, evaporating before they hit the ground. As the gunfire continued, the motorcade of three four-wheel-drives crossed the flat dirt encampment. Scores of bin Laden's most devout followers were here, all carrying Chinese- and Russian-made machine guns. Several were posted strategically with rocket-propelled grenades."

---

the Taliban's support. In return, the Taliban would be given millions of dollars for its military activities.

To Kill the Americans and Their Allies

In 1996 Bin Laden made a declaration of jihad from his new home in southern Afghanistan. He called for all good Muslims to oppose both the United States and Saudi Arabia, saying that "the walls of oppression and humiliation cannot be demolished except in a rain of bullets."[120]

Two years later he called again for jihad—this time from one of his Afghan terrorist camps. "For more than seven years," he said, "the U.S. has been occupying the lands of Islam in the holiest of places, the Arabian peninsula, plundering its riches, dictating to its rulers, humiliating its people, terrorizing its neighbors, and turning its bases in the peninsula into a spearhead through which to fight the neighboring Muslim peoples."[121] It was the duty, he said, for all Muslim people to kill the Americans and their allies—civilian and military—in any country in which it was possible to do so.

Within a short time, terrorists used car bombs against U.S. embassies in Kenya and Tanzania, killing a total of 224 people. Two years later the USS *Cole*, a ship docked in Yemen, was bombed. Seventeen crew members died in that attack. Though Bin Laden would not say whether al Qaeda operatives were responsible, he made no secret of the fact that he was delighted by the results. In fact, at the wedding of one of his sons, he sang a song he had written about the bombing: "The pieces of the bodies of the infidels were flying like dust particles. If you had seen it with your own eyes, your heart would have been filled with joy."[122]

The Afghan Camps

By standing up to the United States and its allies, Osama bin Laden became a hero to many young men in Afghanistan and in other Muslim nations. The al Qaeda camps soon filled with recruits eager to play a role in the jihad. Not every camp specialized in terrorist tactics; in fact, the first set of lessons was to teach the men basic fighting techniques.

Although the camps had enough money to reproduce lesson packets—complete with illustrations and diagrams—for each student, they chose to teach in the ancient method of repetition. Students slowly and methodically copied each lesson in longhand—as one U.S. military expert noted, "like a monk in a monastery in the Middle Ages."[123] If the lesson was written sloppily or incorrectly, the instructor would make the student start again until it was perfect. This method stressed self-discipline and patience, and by copying the lesson himself, the student was taught to remember each word.

The infantry camp lasted a few weeks, and students were taught the basics of light weapons, demolition, and communications. The students learned with weapons and ammunition that were supplied by the Taliban. After mastering this material, students were often ordered to fight with the Taliban soldiers against the resistance. In a few weeks they would return to the camp, and instructors would decide who was to be allowed to continue to the next level.

Although al Qaeda did not take credit for the 2000 terrorist attack on the USS Cole, an American ship docked in Yemen, Bin Laden publicly praised the attack.

Advanced Terrorism Courses

Very ambitious, skilled recruits at the al Qaeda camps in Afghanistan were offered specialized courses in terrorism. In their *New York Times* article "Turning Out Guerrillas and Terrorists to Wage a Holy War," C.J. Chivers and David Rohde explain how such a class was set up.

"Although standard jihad training prepared recruits for ground combat, the line between guerrilla and terrorist could often grow fuzzy. Basic courses provided a martial foundation, and government officials said that with initiative and further study, the graduates could develop specialized terrorist skills, much as Timothy McVeigh, once a conventional American infantryman, later built the truck bomb that killed 168 people in Oklahoma City.

Al-Qaeda and other groups did not leave this evolution entirely to chance. They were trying to do more than use guerrilla insurgents to topple Muslim governments they saw as secular or corrupt. They had declared war against infidels and were eager to carry the battle to where the infidels lived.

To further this end, students with special abilities were identified in basic camps and sent to courses that prepared them for more difficult missions. . . . Only a very small fraction of the jihadis are thought to have received the higher level of training, government officials say, but it was enough to improve the guerrilla forces and to turn loose a resourceful breed of killer on the larger world.

'Afghanistan,' said [one State Department expert], 'was the swamp these terrorists kept coming out of.'"

"You Need to Be a Normal Person"

The decision to allow a student to continue into the terrorist camp was made not only because of his skill in the first part of the course but also because of his religious fervor. In fact, religion was such a key part of the curriculum that the terrorist camp began each day in the same way—a call to prayer for all the men, followed by religious discussions about Islam and their role as Muslim soldiers. One student terrorist, who had spent time at two camps in Afghanistan, explained, "The main purpose of the course was to make a strong group of terrorists within the framework of Islam. The people who had been working with the Taliban from the beginning, they chose the students for the Special Course in Terrorism. We students had to be more religious than others."[124]

Besides religious study, student terrorists were taught the basics of covert operations among the enemy—in this case, the United States and its allies. They were taught that the only way to be successful was to learn to slip in and out of an enemy country like ghosts. "You need to be a normal person," explained one student. "If you go with beard and Islamic dress, the intelligence officer . . . [will] want to ask a lot of questions."[125]

"Playing with Balloons"

It was often difficult for fundamentalist Muslims to change the appearance they believed to be crucial to their faith. But whereas growing a beard and dressing as a Muslim were appropriate in a country such as Afghanistan, it was imperative that they blend in when in a Western nation. FBI and other intelligence agencies would be less suspicious of a Middle Eastern–looking man if he were clean shaven, smoking a cigarette, and wearing cologne—especially the latter. "The cologne," explained one former student, "would make them think, 'I like smelling good for women.'"[126]

The students were also encouraged to use codes when communicating with other terrorists. Because the United States and other nations have the capacity to wiretap or otherwise monitor telephone conversations, it was important to refrain from using suspicious words. For example, they were taught to say "Canada" when they meant "Afghanistan," and "a sick friend" when they were referring to a fellow terrorist who had been detained or arrested. "Playing with balloons" was code for the all-important "fighting a jihad."

The terrorist camps, like the infantry camps, were set up like any college or university, with the day broken into various subjects. Students learned about kidnapping, killing police or security officers, and surveilling assassination targets. One way in which they learned was by studying failed attempts, such

Graduates from al Qaeda training camps, like these who serve as Bin Laden's personal bodyguards, were well trained in combat techniques as well as terrorist tactics.

as the attempted killing of Egyptian president Hosni Mubarak in June 1995. After they reviewed the specifics of a failed attempt, students broke into smaller groups to discuss the reason for the failure—communication among the terrorists, a change of plans by the target, and so on.

Poisoning Dogs

Students were taught to identify the most important structural targets in a country and to plan their destruction. One terrorist, who had spent time in the Khalden camp in the mountains of Afghanistan, explained that the types of targets were "such installations as electric plants, gas plants, airports, railroads, large corporations, gas, gas installations, and millitary installations . . . [as well as] hotels where conferences are held."[127]

Ahmed Ressam, who was arrested in 1999 for trying to enter the United States from Canada in a car loaded with explosives, told authorities that he had learned a great deal in his camp about using poison as a weapon, too. Ressam's teachers used small dogs to demonstrate the effects of certain poisons. In the following excerpt from a cross-examination, Ressam was asked about such demonstrations involving the poisonous compound cyanide:

> Q: Your chief put cyanide in the box [with a dog], is that correct?
>
> A: Yes.
>
> Q: He added sulphuric acid to the cyanide, correct?
>
> A: Yes.

Q: And the dog shortly thereafter died from that experiment, correct?

A: Correct.

Q: How long in general would you say that you watched these dogs suffer?

A: Not very long. . . . I don't remember precisely, maybe four minutes, because the dog was very small. . . .

Q: You practiced these techniques on the dogs so that later on in one of your operations you would be able to perform such techniques on human beings, is that correct?

A: Yes. We wanted to know what is the effect of the gas, yes.[128]

"God Almighty Has Ordered Us"

Western terrorism experts acknowledge that the written lessons used in the camps were both extremely detailed and well organized. The material was presented in exactly the same way in a variety of languages and dialects, so there would be no confusion or inconsistency from one camp to another. "Wherever they got this, it was modeled after somebody's program," said one expert. "It was not made by some guys on some goat farm outside Kabul."[129]

The material was very complete; it taught students that there was usually more than one way to create terror in a given situation. For example, one manual showed students how to concoct their own explosives and poisons when usual ingredients were scarce. Textbooks found in Afghan camps explain how to create explosive boosters beginning with a paste made from warm water and aspirin.

And throughout the written lessons there were constant reminders that the destruction and killing the students were learning were ordained by God. In one explosives manual, the authors assure the students in the preface that they are following divine orders:

> God Almighty has ordered us to terrorize his enemies. In compliance with God's order and his Prophet's order, in an attempt to get out of the humiliation in which we have found ourselves, we shall propose to those who are keen on justice, fighting against those who oppose them and those who diminish them until they receive fresh orders from God. To those alone, we present: Rudimentary Methods in the Manufacturing of Explosive Materials Effective for Demolition purposes.[130]

"So Many of Them Are Willing to Die"

The greatness of becoming a martyr, of dying for Islam, was thoroughly ingrained in their studies—an idea that U.S. terrorism experts found frightening. Because the student terrorists were taught to make plans that did not necessitate their own escape, this brand of terrorism was extremely difficult to prevent.

Pages from an al Qaeda training manual show detailed instructions for building bombs and laying land mines.

Robert Bryant, former deputy director of the FBI, admitted that the United States had not faced this ideology before. "What makes [Bin Laden's] group different from [others] we've seen before . . . is that so many of them are willing to die,"[131] he said. Bin Laden himself was proud of this fact, bragging to a U.S. reporter, "Youths [in his camps] only want one thing, to kill you so they can go to paradise."[132]

One of the last assignments a student had to complete at his camp was to make a suicide video—a personal message proclaiming his devotion to Islam and his hatred for the United States and its allies. The video would be played for his family and his fellow students after he died in a mission—something that all students had been taught to eagerly anticipate.

"Children . . . Are the Best Tools"

The students who studied in the al Qaeda camps at the time of the Taliban came from a variety of backgrounds. Many came from Arab nations, such as Sudan and Saudi Arabia, where fundamentalist Islam was taught in religious schools. The Afghans who flocked to the camps tended to be products of the refugee camps, where poverty and violence were a way of life.

One UN representative warned of the dangers that economic hardships on the heels of decades of war could produce. "You are talking about two generations of children and youth who have been exposed to war nonstop," he noted. "Unless the children have viable alternatives, Afghanistan will be an incubator that can be exploited or manipulated by almost anyone."[133]

His words rang true; no "viable alternatives" presented themselves through the Taliban. Instead, violence and economic woes made families more desperate and angry with their situation in life. It was not surprising that hundreds of Afghanistan's teens and young men were recruited by both the Taliban and its terror arm, al Qaeda.

One Taliban official claimed that children were almost preferable to adults as soldiers, for they could more easily be molded to their recruiter's anti-American viewpoint. "Children are innocent," he explained, "so they are the best tools against dark forces."[134] And of all the children, war orphans were best. Not only would they look to the Taliban as their new family, but in case the children had second thoughts, they had no home to which to flee.

In a "Modern" Madrassa

Just as during the war with the Soviets, many of Afghanistan's refugee children attended madrassas. A great many of these religious schools were in Pakistan. Although these boys—age seven and up—were not being taught terrorism, in quite a few of the madrassas they were certainly learning the most militant interpretation of Islam.

Haqqania, the largest of the madrassas in Pakistan, was a good example. It was spread over eight acres and had room for almost three thousand students. Just as during the Soviet war, when the future Taliban officials attended madrassas, Afghan refugees were offered free room and board. Not surprisingly, many parents in the camps—desperate for their sons to have something to do—were more than willing to send their boys to Haqqania.

Reporter Jeffrey Goldberg from *New York Times Magazine* visited the madrassa in 1999. He found that there was very little change in the curriculum from twenty-five years before; for example, he observed classes of boys memorizing the Koran in Arabic even though none of them spoke that language. Some of the boys were studying to be *muftis*, clerics who are permitted to make religious rulings or declarations of jihad.

"We Would Kill Americans"

Besides memorizing the Koran, boys were instructed in an extremely militant form of Islam. The Taliban soldiers were legends to the boys, as were al Qaeda fighters and Osama bin Laden. Goldberg recalled that as he strolled the grounds of the madrassa, two eleven-year-old boys liked to "jump out from behind a hiding place, scream 'Osama!' and pretend to shoot me."[135]

Talking with the students, many of whom were Afghan boys, Goldberg found that they held strong viewpoints about the relationship

A Day at a Madrassa

For his *New York Times Magazine* article "The Education of a Holy Warrior," reporter Jeffrey Goldberg spent time talking to boys at a madrassa in Pakistan. Some of the boys' responses to his questions startled him, as he explains.

"I then asked: Who wants to see Osama bin Laden armed with nuclear weapons? Every hand in the room shot up. The students laughed and some applauded. But, I said, innocent people would inevitably die if the bomb was used. Even if the West, or Russia, is subjugating Muslims, does that give bin Laden and his supporters the right to kill innocent people?

'Osama has never killed anybody innocent,' one student, whose name was Ghazi, answered.

'What if you were shown proof that he did?'

'The Americans say they have proof, but they don't give it to the Taliban.' . . .

I then took from my notebook . . . the 1998 fatwa issued by bin Laden's organization. . . . I read them a passage, the English translation of which reads as follows: 'The ruling to kill the Americans and their allies—civilians and military—is an individual duty for every Muslim who can do it in any country in which it is possible to do it.'. . .

Here it is, I said, in black and white: bin Laden calling for the death of all Americans, civilian and military.

'Osama didn't write that,' one student yelled, and the others cheered. 'That's a forgery of the Americans.'"

Young boys pose at the window of their madrassa, where they are taught a militant interpretation of Islam.

Osama bin Laden persuaded the Taliban to destroy this ancient Buddhist statue and several others in the village of Bamlyan.

between Islam and the West. In fact, he noted, because of their poor upbringing and their fundamentalist teachers, they had become "the perfect jihad machine."[136] One boy insisted, "Osama bin Laden is a great Muslim. The West is afraid of strong Muslims, so they made him their enemy. Osama wants to keep Islam pure from the pollution of the infidels. He believes Islam is the way for all the world. He wants to bring Islam to all the world."[137] Other students expressed their hope that they would be allowed to die for their religion—hopefully

after killing many U.S. citizens. "We would sacrifice our lives for Osama," one youngster said. "We would kill Americans. All Americans."[138]

"How Will I Explain Myself to God?"

Some members of the Taliban were concerned about their growing interdependence with Bin Laden and al Qaeda. At first, one official later explained, the Taliban made their own decisions on what they believed was best for Afghanistan. However, as soon as Bin Laden took up residence in Afghanistan, he began to take control, largely because of the money he offered them. The official admitted that such generosity was hard for the Taliban to turn down. "Sometimes [Osama] would walk in," he said, "take out a lot of money (as much as $100,000 at a time) and give it to everyone."[139]

Others insisted that the Taliban became far more strict after Bin Laden became involved, too. It was Bin Laden and al Qaeda, one official said, who persuaded Mohammad Omar that it was his Islamic duty to destroy the ancient Buddha statues in Bamlyan, which had stood long before Islam had come to the region. The destruction of the eight-hundred-year-old statues was condemned throughout the world, including in Islamic nations.

Many devout Muslims in Afghanistan even begged Omar to reconsider because the giant carved statues were a national treasure. However, Omar would not reconsider. "If even one Muslim prays before the Buddhas," he wondered aloud, "how will I explain myself to God?"[140]

"We Are Your Tigers"

There was no question that the Taliban was soundly behind al Qaeda and its terrorist goals. Not only did it recruit for Bin Laden, but it also was willing to shield him from law enforcement agencies that considered him a threat to the world. Al Qaeda was grateful to Mullah Omar, too, for allowing it the freedom to establish its facilities in Afghanistan with full governmental cooperation. One terrorist fighter, in a poem dedicated to the Taliban, wrote, "We are your tigers here in the black mountain."[141]

But the militant brand of Islam—especially the terrorism aimed at the United States and its allies—was not popular with many Afghan people. True, they were angry with the United States for using Afghanistan during the war with the Soviets. As one man challenged, "The West had use for us when the Soviets invaded our land in 1979, when we were a front line in the Cold War. We were worth helping then. We are not so important now."[142] Like many Afghans, he felt that many of Afghanistan's problems after the war could have been solved by foreign aid and interest by the West. However, there was no excuse for the terrorism perpetrated against America—especially those acts committed against civilians by al Qaeda operatives in New York and Washington, D.C., on September 11, 2001. One Kabul resident spoke out against that terrorism, which was supported by his government. "Why must so many people die?" he wondered. "It doesn't matter who they are; they all have a mother and a father."[143]

Resistance to the Taliban

Even as the Taliban was growing in power, however, the Afghan people resisted the regime in many ways. Although some of this resistance involved hundreds—even thousands—of Afghan people, many examples of effective resistance occurred almost every day on a smaller scale.

"They Haven't Crushed Our Spirit"

One form of resistance centered around the burka; although women wore it, many of them despised it. Women who, before the Taliban came to power, were doctors, lawyers, or teachers and were used to wearing business suits found that they felt invisible in the baglike garment.

Although refusing to wear the burka would certainly have resulted in a beating or imprisonment, some women found pleasure in visiting an "underground" beauty parlor. Of course, the operation was illegal because the women who ran it were not supposed to be working—and because nail polish and makeup were taboo. One burka-clad reporter who visited the secret operation wondered about the wisdom of risking punishment for one's appearance. "[The operator] had a beauty table with all the makeup laid out—hairsprays, lipstick, everything," she wrote. "She knew she'd go to prison for doing it. I could understand people risking everything for education—but for beauty?"[144]

Indeed, rather than appearing fearful of being caught, the women visiting the secret shop were defiant. One said she had always been used to looking her best, but the Taliban had made that impossible—at least on the outside. Perhaps it was not important to everyone, but for her, it made a difference. By having her hair done and her nails manicured, she felt some measure of her old self. The beauty operator agreed. "You can make a woman wear a veil," she stated, "but this is our way of showing that they haven't crushed our spirit."[145]

"Their Eyes Open Very Wide"

Another Afghan, a man known as Jahan Mir, risked imprisonment by repairing televisions. The Taliban had banned television and had destroyed every broadcasting station in Afghanistan to ensure there were no programs to watch. Of course, people could pick up foreign stations if they had the proper equipment, but that would involve a satellite dish, which would have been too obvious. Televisions equipped with DVD attachments could play movies, however. Those were also banned because many movies were made in Western, non-Islamic nations and because, like television shows, movies included pictures of the human form, which was against the Taliban's interpretation of the Koran.

Afghan people wanted to watch movies, however, and Mir was willing to risk certain prison time by making sure that their sets worked. He estimated that more than 25 percent of Afghans watched movies, and many of them were members of the Taliban. "Some of the Taliban watch . . . even a few commanders," he said. "Their eyes open very wide, and they remember everything. They can tell you exactly where they were when they were watching what movie."[146]

was taking, especially if a border guard were to find the smuggled movies in his car. He felt that it was worth the risk, however, because the movies provided some relief from the dull lives under the Taliban. He also felt a secret pleasure in fooling the Taliban. "Yes," he said. "I think I am someone brave."[148]

Many Afghans defied the law of sharia in a variety of ways. Although they are clad in burkas, these women risk punishment for openly displaying a poster of a cat in their home.

"I Think I Am Someone Brave"

Anyone whom the Taliban's PVPV police caught with a movie would be jailed for three or four months. Some movie-possession arrests resulted in stiffer sentences, however. "If they find you with a sex movie," Mir said, "that's much worse, three years in jail. This is very bad because most American films have sex. You are better off watching kung fu movies or Rambo, or movies from India, which are very popular."[147]

In addition to repairing his customers' television sets, Mir made the five-hour drive into Pakistan on a regular basis. In Pakistan he could buy many new movies for a reasonable price—the equivalent of a few dollars. People often pooled their money and bought films so that the cost was not prohibitive.

Mir said that he worried sometimes about the risk he

One of the Last Girls' Schools

Numerous Afghan people took great risks as teachers and pupils during the time of the Taliban. Despite the war raging around them, in the northern village of Taliqan many girls bravely attended one of the last schools still open to them. Taliqan was held by a resistance army most of the time, and the Taliban's army was never far away. "The war, of course, is the biggest problem that we face," said the school's headmistress. "Sometimes, parents prefer that their children should stay at home to work and support the family, rather than go to school."[149]

The school reflected the violence around it. It had no windows, no chairs or desks, and its walls had been strafed by bullets. Even so, about two hundred students sat on the floor, balancing their papers on their knees as they learned to read and to study science, math, and history. The headmistress felt strongly about the school's mission and was worried about what would happen if the area was finally taken over by the Taliban. "To deprive women of education is to deprive half of society of education. . . . The war is taking a terrible toll here," she said, "leaving us almost without hope."[150]

More Discretion in the City

Although girls were at risk in Taliqan, they did not have to be secretive about being students. But in the 90 percent of Afghanistan that was firmly under Taliban control, schools still functioned. The difference, of course, was that the schools and the students and their teachers had to be far more discreet.

It would attract attention, for example, if a large group of children were seen entering a house or apartment at the same time. One woman, who had been a high school science teacher before the Taliban took power, was asked to tutor several girls secretly in her home. She agreed but was worried when "several girls" grew to become fifteen to eighteen girls. She knew the Taliban PVPV police would notice that many girls, especially if they carried notebooks. She finally solved the problem by having the girls come in shifts of four, every two hours.

Younger girls—age ten and under—did not raise a great deal of suspicion among the Taliban. But older girls, says one expert, were watched carefully by the police as they moved about the villages and cities; as a result, there was little prospect of continuing their lessons after age ten. "Girls above ten have been beaten by the vice and virtue police for trying to study," she says, "so access to secondary education is extremely dangerous and virtually non-existent."[151]

The secret schools had no textbooks or supplies and got by only on the meager donations of the girls' parents. Even so, the girls were excited about their progress. "I like all the lessons," said one girl. "It's useful for my family. If my father gives me some money to buy something, I'm able to count the change." For her parents, there was an even greater reward—seeing their daughter think about having choices about her future. "I never had the opportunity to go to school myself," says her mother. "I would like her in the future to be a doctor or an engineer or a teacher."[152]

Not Only Girls

Girls were not the only students forced to be secretive. Many boys attended underground schools, too, although for different reasons. Though the Taliban permitted boys to attend school, there were no choices about curriculum. Schools were to teach the Koran primarily and little else—just as the Taliban leaders had been educated years ago in their madrassas.

Many parents of boys were glad that their children would receive an education, but they were concerned by the fundamentalist nature of the religious studies. They also were unhappy that their sons would not be

Secret School

Batya Swift Yasgur's *Behind the Burqa: Our Life in Afghanistan and How We Escaped to Freedom* is sisters Hala and Sulima's account of daily life under the Taliban. In this excerpt, Hala describes the secret school that she started and its tragic results.

"I was sitting in the front room of the second floor. We called that room the 'office' because that was where we handed out assignments to the children. I looked out the window onto the courtyard, and there they were. Four of them [Taliban] this time. All with guns. . . .

Today they didn't knock. They pushed against the door and stormed through the house. Two of them grabbed my hair and pulled me down the stairs and into the court-

yard. . . . [One man] pulled my hair harder and the other man slapped me. 'We know who you are. You come from a family of infidels. . . . Lying and heresy run in your blood.' The other man slapped me again. . . .

I do not remember all the rest. I remember the pain. I remember the blows. I remember the feeling of fists against my cheek. Of hair being wrenched from my scalp. The sound of a woman crying. The sound of children shrieking. The sound of the men shouting, 'Children, go home. If we ever catch any one of you in this house again, we will burn down the house with you in it.'

The next thing I knew, I was being pulled to my feet by my hair. 'You deserve to die,' one of the men said."

Some Afghan teachers risked their lives to operate secret schools where boys and girls were taught a well-rounded, non-fundamentalist curriculum.

able to receive a more well-rounded education, with history, mathematics, science, or languages. These parents, too, looked for secret schools where their sons could study alongside girls. By the summer of 2001, it was estimated that there were forty-five thousand children—about one-fourth of them boys—studying in Afghanistan's secret schools.

At Kabul University, young medical students—all men—often took risks in their own form of disobedience. The Taliban had created strict rules for young men studying to be doctors, and one of these rules prohibited the use of cadavers and skeletons in anatomy classes. This caused problems for the stu-

dents, who felt that only by studying real bodies could they truly understand how the various systems of the body worked.

"I Felt Bad Taking His Skeleton"

One young man, Karim Ahmed, was very worried that his studies, which were limited to pictures in books, were teaching him nothing. He made the decision to dig up a skeleton in the cemetery and take it home so he could study the bones and their relationship to one another. When he arrived in the cemetery with his shovel and flashlight, he was

Pictured is a student at a secret school operated by the Revolutionary Association of the Women of Afghanistan. During the Taliban regime, RAWA worked to provide women with education and health care.

happy to find the headstone of a former neighbor.

Although Ahmed knew it was wrong to dig up the body, he felt that the benefits might eventually outweigh the wrong he committed. "Naturally, I felt bad about taking his skeleton," he said. "But the Taliban said using skeletons was not allowed by Islam, so I had no choice. I thought that if twenty people could benefit from his skeleton, it would be good."[153] As it turned out, Ahmed scored extremely high on his medical exams, and his fellow students followed his example and began robbing graves to study, too.

RAWA

Some resistance to the Taliban was formally organized. One of the most important resistance groups, and arguably the best-known opponent of fundamental Islam and the Taliban, was the Revolutionary Association of the Women of Afghanistan (RAWA). Surprisingly, RAWA was not started in response to the Taliban government. It was started in 1977 by a group of nurses and students who wanted to force their conservative Muslim society to give more rights to women.

A young woman calling herself "Behjat" (RAWA members are often in such danger that they cannot go by their real names) said that, at first, the group was criticized by society for using the word *revolutionary*. Critics insisted that the word frightened people. "Many times people tell us to get rid of the word . . . in our name," Behjat said. "But what is revolutionary is calling for women's rights. What is revolutionary is calling for education and democracy. So, yes, we support what is revolutionary in today's Afghanistan. We won't compromise our policies."[154]

The founders of RAWA had no idea that Afghanistan would take such leaps backward in terms of women's rights three decades after the organization began. Since the Taliban came to power in 1996, RAWA's two thousand members worked hard, and at great peril, to establish schools for girls and health centers for women that operated under the Taliban's radar.

The Khaiwa Camp

RAWA was most proud of its camps in Pakistan, which included hospitals, schools, and orphanages. Of course, these facilities were run in secret because many fundamentalist Muslims lived in the area and had strong ties to the Taliban. A careless word to one of them could have resulted in the shutting down of a facility and even the death of a RAWA worker.

One camp in which secrecy was not needed was a refugee camp in northwestern Pakistan near the Afghanistan border. Called Khaiwa, it was situated in a quarry in order to avoid the Taliban soldiers who frequented refugee camps looking for army recruits. Because of its location, Khaiwa offered privacy for its five hundred families. The camp was started during the Soviet war by one of the rare progressive mujahideen. He believed that education should be universal and hired RAWA workers to teach and counsel the families traumatized by the war. During the Taliban regime, it was a lifesaver for many women and girls.

Khaiwa's refugees did not wear burkas or hide the fact that their camp provided orphanages, schools for girls, and health care for everyone who needed it. One of the camp's teachers said that her experience at the camp was more rewarding than in other schools. "My oldest student is 45 years old," she explained. "She's so happy now to be able to read letters from her relatives. She told me, 'I now know the pleasure of eyes.'"[155]

Although the Khaiwa camp was safe, other refugee camps at which RAWA sponsored clinics and schools reported violence against the workers. Teachers' offices were burned, clinics had equipment smashed or stolen, and many RAWA workers received anonymous telephone messages threatening them with physical harm. One woman said she had received so many death threats from the Taliban that she simply replied, "You know where I am. I won't stop what I'm doing."[156]

Even with such risks, however, RAWA workers felt that their work was too crucial to stop. "It makes our commitment stronger," said one worker in a Pakistan camp. "I will work with RAWA until the end of my life. My desire is to return as a free woman to a peaceful and democratic Afghanistan."[157]

Disposable Cameras and the Internet

One of RAWA's most important accomplishments during the Taliban's rule was to alert the rest of the world to the atrocities that were occurring daily in Afghanistan. Though the Afghan people were aware of the cruel and inhumane methods of punishment under the Taliban, for example, most people in other nations had no idea of what the Afghans were enduring.

The association's methods were simple—RAWA volunteers would take as many pictures documenting atrocities as they could without getting caught—for, of course, photography was illegal under the Taliban. Ironically, however, the hated burka provided the means to take pictures secretly; women could hide the cameras beneath the heavy

"Someday We Will Die"

Sajeda Hayat and Sehar Saba (not their real names), leaders of RAWA, gave an interview to Katha Pollitt of New York Times Magazine in May 2000. In the following excerpt, the two women discuss their feelings about the dangerous lives they lead.

"[POLLITT:] Do some . . . say you should lead more conventional lives?

HAYAT: Oh, yeah. They say I'm young, I should be thinking about nice things, enjoy life . . . think about fashion. I say, sure, but how can you think about clothes when people are being raped and killed, and they're so poor they're selling their children on the streets? Maybe some people could think about fashion, but we can't.

[POLLITT:] Do you [RAWA members] talk among yourselves about the harm that might befall you?

HAYAT: Of course. We make jokes, we pretend to make up our wills. Older, more experienced members say we should have all preparations. But we don't talk much about it. When you think about what's going on in Afghanistan, you stop caring so much about your own safety. And we have ways of staying cheerful. We read books by women who've been brave—Iranian, Vietnamese, even Joan of Arc. If I get depressed and lose hope, then what will other women and girls my age have to look to?

SABA: If the Taliban caught me inside Afghanistan, they would definitely torture and kill me, stone me as a quote-unquote prostitute. So the punishment has already been decreed. But I can do it. I'm ready for anything. Someday we will die, but maybe it will be a prouder death than from some natural cause."

Using a hidden camera, RAWA members filmed a Taliban police officer beating two women for removing their burkas in public. Such horrific images exposed the atrocities of the Taliban to the world.

veil and shoot through the small mesh opening.

After taking pictures of an event, RAWA volunteers would bring the cameras to Pakistan, where they would publish the pictures on the organization's Web site. It was the Internet, say RAWA leaders, that really enabled them to show the world what was happening in Afghanistan. The images are horrifying, and the site warns that some of the pictures may be too graphic for some. In one photo, a grinning boy holds up a string from which two bloody hands dangle. The hands had just been severed in a public amputation. In another photograph, several cheering men watch as a woman is stoned.

One of the Web site's supporters was talk-show host Oprah Winfrey, who did a show about RAWA and its mission. She urged women throughout the United States to donate small, easily concealed cameras to RAWA so it could continue its work. Thousands of viewers did just that. "Through our website, we have made many contacts," said one RAWA leader. "We have gained the support of many dedicated women's groups, activists, and individuals. Some of them are so dedicated, especially in the U.S."[158]

Beneath the Veil

Sometimes visitors to Afghanistan made a difference in resisting the Taliban. A half-Afghan British reporter named Saira Shah traveled to Afghanistan—smuggled in by RAWA workers—in the spring of 2000 to see for herself what was happening there. Shah's goal was to make a documentary that could be shown on television around the world.

She took miles of video footage, interviewing Afghan people who had lost relatives and friends to Taliban soldiers and visiting battlefields where resistance fighters still opposed the Taliban government. She visited a northern village where, just weeks earlier, Taliban forces had brutally murdered dozens of civilians, and she interviewed three teenagers whose mother had been one of the victims. But some of the most shocking footage was not taken by Shah but was donated by the women of RAWA. The footage, notes one viewer, was wobbly but completely arresting:

> A soccer stadium in Afghanistan is packed with people, but there is no match today. Instead, a pickup truck drives into the stadium with three women, shrouded in [burkas], cowering in the back. Armed men in turbans force a woman from the truck, and make her kneel at the penalty line on the field. Confused and unable to see, the woman tries to look behind just as a rifle is pointed against the back of her head.
>
> With no fanfare whatsoever, she is shot dead. The shaky video camera captures the cheering crowd as people rise to their feet, hoping to get a better view of the corpse on the ground.[159]

Shah's documentary, *Beneath the Veil*, was seen on CNN, though other televison networks around the world found the violence contained in it worrisome and decided not to air it. RAWA workers were angered by the decision since Shah and many RAWA volunteers had risked their lives in making the documentary. One RAWA official fumed that networks were more worried about the sensi-

bilities of viewers than the victims of such atrocities. "[The video] was too strong to be aired," she said, "but not too strong to have happened to a woman in Afghanistan."[160] However, even though it was not played widely, the documentary did educate millions of people about the cruel methods of the Taliban.

The Lion of the Panjshir

In addition to taking risks by disobeying Taliban rules and documenting the government's brutality, there was another, more direct type of resistance. Guerrilla fighters who were opposed to the fundamentalist brand of Islam represented by the Taliban had fought against the regime since it first had emerged. The most respected fighter was Ahmed Shah Massoud.

Massoud's forces were what kept the Taliban from controlling the entire nation; at the height of the Taliban's power, it could only boast of ruling 90 percent of Afghanistan. Areas in the west and in the Panjshir Valley, north of Kabul, were strongholds of fighters who continued to resist the Taliban. Because of his dogged refusal to let the Taliban take over the valley, Massoud was respectfully known as "the Lion of the Panjshir."

Writer Sebastian Junger, who spent time with Massoud in the mountains of Afghanistan in 2000, was struck by how brilliant a strategist Massoud was and by how much he cared for the safety of his fighters. As he planned one dangerous raid against the encroaching Taliban, Massoud urged his commanders to select men for the mission who were not married, who had no children, and who were not their families' only sons. As he explained the strategy, Junger noted that "Massoud was so far ahead of his commanders that at times he seemed unable to decide whether to explain his thinking, or to just give them orders and hope for the best."[161]

September 9

Massoud did not believe that his resistance fighters needed to defeat the Taliban—they only had to survive long enough for the Taliban to self-destruct. He knew in 2000 that there was growing hatred of the government because of its rigid fundamentalism and that uprisings throughout the nation would eventually topple the Taliban. There was one aspect of the Taliban government, however, that was extremely troubling to him. He was aware of the growing relationship between the Taliban

Ahmed Shah Massoud

Along with photojournalist Reza Deghati, writer Sebastian Junger spent time with resistance fighter Ahmed Shah Massoud in November 2000. The following excerpt is from a short piece Junger wrote for *National Geographic Adventure* titled "Requiem for a Warrior," after Massoud was killed by al Qaeda terrorists.

"Reza and I sat at his kitchen table with a bottle of wine. Someone had sent him an e-mail that day that said, 'You must be a happy man to have met Ahmad Shah Massoud.' And in fact we both knew we'd been incredibly fortunate to have known him. Massoud—who loathed the extremism of the Taliban as much as he did the totalitarianism of the Soviet Union—once told

me he was fighting not only for a free Afghanistan but for a free world.

There was something about him, the slow nod of his head as he listened to a question, the exhaustion and curiosity engraved on his handsome, haggard face that made it clear we were in the presence of an extraordinary man. I found it impossible not to listen to him when he spoke, even though I didn't understand a word. I watched everything he did, because I had the sense that somehow—in the way he poured his tea, in the way his hands carved the air as he talked—there was some secret to be learned."

Ahmad Shah Massoud (left) leads his band of guerrilla rebels in prayer.

and Osama bin Laden's terrorist forces. Massoud knew, too, that the poverty and despair of Afghanistan were perfect ingredients for the extremist Muslims coming from Pakistan's madrassas.

Massoud had shared these concerns many times with the United States and its allies, hoping for help in rebuilding Afghanistan. "We have told Western countries again and again," he said, "of the dangers of Taliban extremism, of bin Laden and his terrorists."[162] But there was little response from the West, and the troubles in Afghanistan worsened.

On September 9, 2001—just two days before al Qaeda operatives flew jets into the World Trade Center and the Pentagon, Massoud was assassinated by two suicide bombers. Experts say with certainty that the men, who pretended to be reporters filming an interview with Massoud, were al Qaeda terrorists.

Sebastian Junger wrote days after Massoud's death that it was no coincidence that the Lion of the Panjshir was killed before September 11. "It seemed to me," Junger said, "that Osama bin Laden had ordered the

The rubble of New York City's World Trade Center smolders after the September 11, 2001, terrorist attacks. Following the attacks, the United States declared war on Afghanistan and succeeded in toppling the Taliban regime.

attempt on Massoud's life before going ahead with his attacks on New York and Washington. He would not have dared to provoke the U.S. the way he had, I believed, were Massoud still alive to make use of the military aid that might have finally been offered to him."[163]

"The Dog Is the Brother of the Wolf"

The U.S. response to September 11 was to declare a war on terror, beginning with the Taliban government that protected Bin Laden. Once again, the people of Afghanistan found themselves in the middle of a war. This time it involved the United States, a military superpower, attacking the Taliban government, which few Afghan people supported.

Many people fled cities such as Kabul and Kandahar, hoping to protect their families from the bombs. Hundreds of Taliban soldiers fled south to Pakistan, as the U.S.-backed Northern Alliance, a group of anti-Taliban fighters, fought to take back the government. One Afghan woman, exhausted by the violence that had plagued Afghanistan for so long and feeling helpless to protect her children, said, "I pray to God that as soon as America attacks, the first cruise missile hits my house and kills me and my family."[164]

Although Bin Laden remained at large, the Taliban was quickly ousted. However, rather than feeling joy, many Afghan people were wary. The Taliban government was gone, but, as Massoud had often pointed out, thousands of other extremists were pouring out of madrassas in Afghanistan and Pakistan. There were no guarantees that the nation's next leaders would be any different from the harsh Taliban government. One refugee camp worker insisted that until the reasons for such extremism were addressed, there would be no reason for hope that things would be different in Afghanistan. "The devil is the brother of evil," she said. "The dog is the brother of the wolf. We condemn both."[165]

Notes

Introduction: Back to the Dark Ages

1. Zoya, with John Follain and Rita Cristofari, *Zoya's Story: An Afghan Woman's Struggle for Freedom.* New York: William Morrow, 2002, p. 142.
2. Quoted in Zoya, *Zoya's Story*, p. 143.
3. Sally Armstrong, *Veiled Threat: The Hidden Power of the Women of Afghanistan.* New York: Four Walls Eight Windows, 2002, p. 1.

Chapter 1:
The Land of the Great Game

4. Charles H. Norchi, "Blowback from Afghanistan: The Historical Roots," *ciaonet*, February 1996. www.ciaonet.org.
5. Quoted in Ahmed Rashid, *Taliban: Militant Islam, Oil, and Fundamentalism in Central Asia.* New Haven, CT: Yale University Press, 2002, p. 7.
6. Quoted in Norchi, "Blowback from Afghanistan."
7. Quoted in Norchi, "Blowback from Afghanistan."
8. Quoted in Larry Goodson, *Afghanistan's Endless War: State Failure, Regional Politics, and the Rise of the Taliban.* Seattle: University of Washington Press, 2001, p. 56.
9. Sebastian Junger, *Fire.* New York: W.W. Norton, 2001, p. 214.
10. Junger, *Fire*, p. 214.
11. Quoted in Debra Denker, "Along Afghanistan's War-Torn Frontier," *National Geographic*, June 1985, p. 772.
12. Quoted in C.J. Chivers, "Veterans of Soviets' Old War Warn of Betrayal and Brutality," *New York Times*, October 22, 2001, p. B1.
13. Quoted in Robert D. Kaplan, *Soldiers of God: With Islamic Warriors in Afghanistan and Pakistan.* New York: Vintage Departures, 2001, p. 131.
14. Kaplan, *Soldiers of God*, p. 127.
15. Quoted in Kaplan, *Soldiers of God*, p. 2.
16. Quoted in Pankaj Mishra, "The Making of Afghanistan," *New York Review of Books*, November 15, 2001. www.nybooks.com.

Chapter 2:
The Coming of the Taliban

17. Junger, *Fire*, p. 215.
18. Quoted in John Rettie, "Afghan Trail Open Only to VIPs, Liars, and Inspectors," *Manchester Guardian*, August 27, 1993, n.p.
19. Quoted in Marc Kaufman, "Afghan Rules in the Strictest Sense," Knight-Ridder/Tribune News Service, October 12, 1996, n.p.
20. Radek Sikorski, "Killing Time: Kabul, Afghanistan," *Times* (London), September 25, 1993, n.p.
21. Quoted in Rettie, "Afghan Trail Open Only to VIPs, Liars, and Inspectors," n.p.
22. Armstrong, *Veiled Threat*, pp. 6–7.
23. Quoted in Peter Willems, "War Without End," *Middle East*, December 1996, p. 5.
24. Quoted in Sikorski, "Killing Time," n.p.
25. Quoted in Sikorski, "Killing Time," n.p.
26. Quoted in Emily MacFarquhar, "The Rise of Taliban: A New Force of Muslim Fighters Is Determined to Rule Afghanistan," *U.S. News & World Report*,

March 6, 1995, p. 64.

27. Quoted in Kamal Matinuddin, *The Taliban Phenomenon: Afghanistan, 1994–1997*. Oxford, UK: Oxford University Press, 1999, p. 13.

28. Quoted in Tim Judah, "Profile: Mullah Mohammad Omar," *Guardian Unlimited Observer*, September 23, 2001. www.observer.co.uk.

29. Ralph H. Magnus and Eden Naby, *Afghanistan: Mullah, Marx, and Mujahid.* Boulder, CO: Westview, 2002, p. 182.

30. Quoted in Johanna McGeary, "The Taliban Troubles," *Time*, October 1, 2001, p. 38.

31. Zoya, *Zoya's Story*, pp. 128–29.

32. Quoted in Michael Lev, "Holy War Without End," *Chicago Tribune*, November 24, 1996, p. 1.

33. Quoted in Ian MacWilliam, "Afghan Villagers Feel Betrayed by Taliban Zealots," *Plain Dealer*, November 8, 1996, p. 10A.

34. Quoted in Christina Lamb, "Taliban Bring Terror to Refugee Camps," *London Telegraph Online*, September 30, 2001. www.telegraph.co.uk.

35. Quoted in Lamb, "Taliban Bring Terror to Refugee Camps."

36. *Human Rights Watch*, "The Massacre at Mazar-i Sharif," vol. 10, November 1998, n.p.

37. Quoted in Carlotta Gall, "Killings from Taliban's Era Still Haunt a Valley," *New York Times*, July 25, 2002, p. A1.

38. Quoted in Dexter Filkins, "Under Autumn Snow, Footnotes to Village's Sorrowful Decade," *New York Times*, December 9, 2001, p. B1.

Chapter 3: Life Under the Sharia

39. Quoted in *Current Events*, "Storm from the Hills," November 4, 1996, p. 2.

40. Quoted in Kaufman, "Aghan Rules in the Strictest Islamic Sense."

41. Quoted in Andrew Meier, "Stoners," *New Republic*, October 7, 1996, p. 14.

42. Quoted in Christina Lamb, "I Was One of the Taliban's Torturers," *London Telegraph Online*, September 30, 2001. www.telegraph.co.uk.

43. Quoted in Willems, "War Without End," p. 5.

44. Quoted in Michael Lev, "Tyranny of Religion Imperils Rich Culture," *Chicago Tribune*, December 3, 1996, p. 1.

45. Quoted in Lev, "Tyranny of Religion Imperils Rich Culture," p. 1.

46. Quoted in Nadya Labi, "Rhythmless Nation," *Time*, September 15, 2001, p. 60.

47. Quoted in Labi, "Rhythmless Nation," p. 60.

48. Quoted in Lamb, "I Was One of the Taliban's Torturers."

49. Quoted in Lev, "Tyranny of Religion Imperils Rich Culture," p. 1.

50. Quoted in Batya Swift Yasgur, *Behind the Burqa: Our Life in Afghanistan and How We Escaped to Freedom.* Hoboken, NJ: John Wiley & Sons, 2002, p. 202.

51. Quoted in *Wall Street Journal*, "Divided Front?" October 1, 2001, p. A1.

52. Quoted in Labi, "Rhythmless Nation," p. 60.

53. Quoted in Khalid Hasan, "The Taliban's World," *Hindunet*, March 19, 2001. www.hvk.org.

54. Quoted in Scott Johnson, "Love Under the Taliban," *Newsweek International*, April 1, 2002, p. 56.

55. Quoted in Johnson, "Love Under the Taliban," p. 56.

56. Quoted in Erik Eckholm, "Taliban Justice: Stadium Was Scene of Gory

Punishment," *New York Times*, December 26, 2001, p. B1.

57. Quoted in Hasan, "The Taliban's World."

58. Eckholm, "Taliban Justice," p. B1.

59. Quoted in *Chicago Tribune*, "In the Name of Islam, Couple Stoned to Death," November 3, 1996, p. 6.

60. Quoted in Eckholm, "Taliban Justice," p. B1.

61 Quoted in Lamb, "I Was One of the Taliban's Torturers."

62. Quoted in Lamb, "I Was One of the Taliban's Torturers."

63. Quoted in Willems, "War Without End," p. 5.

Chapter 4: Women Under the Taliban

64. Quoted in Rosemarie Skaine, *The Women of Afghanistan Under the Taliban.* Jefferson, NC: McFarland, 2002, p. 22.

65. Quoted in Skaine, *The Women of Afghanistan*, p. 61.

66. Quoted in Armstrong, *Veiled Threat*, p. 4.

67. Quoted in *Sunday Mirror*, "The West at War," September 30, 2001, p. 8.

68. Quoted in Armstrong, *Veiled Threat*, p. 2.

69. Quoted in Kim Willsher, "Prisoners of the Burqa," *Times* (London), October 5, 2001, p. 2.

70. Quoted in Skaine, *The Women of Afghanistan*, p. 43.

71. Quoted in William Maley, ed., *Fundamentalism Reborn? Afghanistan and the Taliban.* New York: New York University Press, 2001, p. 163.

72. Latifa, *My Forbidden Face: Growing Up Under the Taliban: A Young Woman's Story.* New York: Hyperion, 2001, p. 48.

73. Quoted in Armstrong, *Veiled Threat*, pp. 4–5.

74. Quoted in Amanda Ward, "Behind the Veil of Terror," *Daily Mirror*, June 21, 2001, p. 46.

75. Quoted in *Time*, "About Face," December 3, 2001, p. 34.

76. Quoted in Mavis Leno, "The World Needs to Know the Awful Plight of Afghan Women," *Chicago Tribune*, November 1, 1998, p. 8.

77. Quoted in *Bloomington Pantagraph* (IL), "In Afghanistan, Head-to-Toe Garment Hides Identity, Outrage," October 30, 1996, p. A2.

78. Quoted in *Pantagraph*, "In Afghanistan, Head-to-Toe Garment Hides Identity, Outrage," p. A2.

79. Quoted in Anthony Spaeth, "A Peace That Terrifies," *Time*, October 14, 1996, p. 62.

80. Quoted in Sajida Hayat, "Kabul: The City Where Even the Sunrise and Sunset Have Been Upset for a Long Time," *RAWA Online*, January 2000. www.rawa.org.

81. Quoted in *Time*, "About Face," p. 34.

82. Skaine, *The Women of Afghanistan*, p. 66.

83. Quoted in *Sunday Mirror*, "The West at War," p. 8.

84. Quoted in Ward, "Behind the Veil of Terror," p. 46.

85. Christiane Amanpour, "Tyranny of the Taliban," *Time*, October 13, 1997, p. 60.

86. Quoted in Skaine, *The Women of Afghanistan*, p. 72.

87. Quoted in Abbas Faiz, "Health Care Under the Taliban," *Lancet*, April 26, 1997, p. 1,247.

88. Quoted in Skaine, *The Women of Afghanistan*, p. 72.

89. Quoted in Armstrong, *Veiled Threat*, p. 113.

90. Quoted in Armstrong, *Veiled Threat*, pp. 9–10.

91. Quoted in Leslie Mackay, "On Seeing

the Face of an Afghan Woman," *Moxie Magazine Online*, 2001. www.moxie mag.com.

92. Quoted in Skaine, *The Women of Afghanistan*, p. 64.

93. Quoted in Skaine, *The Women of Afghanistan*, p. 65.

Chapter 5: A Life of Grinding Poverty

94. Quoted in Willems, "War Without End," p. 5.

95. Quoted in Amy Waldman, "No TV, No Chess, No Kites," *New York Times*, November 22, 2001, p. A1.

96. *Time*, "Frozen in Time," May 29, 2000, p. 36.

97. Quoted in Pam Constable, "Cold and Hungry in Kabul," *Washington Post*, December 19, 1999, p. 31.

98. Quoted in Constable, "Cold and Hungry in Kabul," p. 31.

99. Quoted in Peter Willems, "Principles at a Price," *Middle East*, March 1997, p. 10.

100. Quoted in Barry Bearak, "An Afghan Mosaic of Misery," *New York Times*, February 25, 2000, p. A1.

101. Bearak, "An Afghan Mosaic of Misery," p. A1.

102. Barry Bearak, "Afghans Ruled by Taliban: Poor, Isolated, but Secure," *New York Times*, October 10, 1998, p. A1.

103. Quoted in Pam Constable, "Afghanistan Struggling to Rebuild," *Washington Post*, October 3, 1998, p. A13.

104. Quoted in Scott Baldauf, "Afghan Path," *Christian Science Monitor*, April 9, 2001, p. 7.

105. Quoted in Baldauf, "Afghan Path," p. 7.

106. Quoted in Baldauf, "Afghan Path," p. 7.

107. Quoted in *Time International*, "End of the Line," February 26, 2001, p. 18.

108. John Sifton, "A Last Road Trip Through Premodern Afghanistan," *Peace Pledge Union*, September 30, 2001. www.ppu. org.uk.

109. Quoted in Shugofa Noori Kabir, "Cloaked in Danger," *Teen Magazine*, August 1999, p. 90.

110. Quoted in Diane Taylor, "Real Lives," *Daily Mirror*, March 24, 2001, p. 2B.

111. Quoted in Amir Shah, "Afghan Refugees Swamp Pakistan Border," *San Diego Union-Tribune*, November 29, 2000, p. A15.

112. Quoted in Chris de Bellaique, "When the Price of Security Is a Life of Poverty," *Independent*, January 10, 2001, p. 16.

113. Quoted in de Bellaique, "When the Price of Security Is a Life of Poverty," p. 16.

114. Quoted in Peter Willems, "Afghanistan's Gold," *Middle East*, September 1997, p. 6.

115. Quoted in Willems, "Afghanistan's Gold," p. 6.

116. Quoted in *USA Today*, "US Expected to Target Afghanistan's Opium," October 16, 2001, p. A1.

117. Quoted in Rashid, *Taliban*, p. 118.

Chapter 6: A Training Ground for Terrorism

118. Quoted in Rashid, *Taliban*, pp. 132–33.

119. S. Amjad Hussain, *The Taliban and Beyond: A Close Look at the Afghan Nightmare*. Perrysburg, OH: BWD, 2001, p. 85.

120. Quoted in Hussain, *The Taliban and Beyond*, p. 85.

121. Quoted in Rashid, *Taliban*, p. 134.

122. Quoted in Lisa Beyer, "The Most Wanted Man in the World," *Time*, September 24, 2001, p. 54.

123. Quoted in C.J. Chivers and David Rohde, "Turning Out Guerrillas and Terrorists to Wage a Holy War," *New York Times*, March 18, 2002, p. A1.

124. Quoted in Scott Baldauf, "Inside a Taliban Terrorism Class," *Christian Science Monitor*, May 6, 2003, p. 6.

125. Quoted in Mark Fineman and Stephen Braun, "Life Inside Al-Qaeda: A Destructive Devotion," *Los Angeles Times*, September 24, 2001, p. A1.

126. Quoted in Fineman and Braun, "Life Inside Al-Qaeda," p. A1.

127. Quoted in *PBS Frontline*, "Trail of a Terrorist," www.pbs.org.

128. Quoted in *PBS Frontline*, "Trail of a Terrorist."

129. Quoted in Chivers and Rohde, "Turning Out Guerrillas and Terrorists to Wage a Holy War," p. A1.

130. Quoted in Chivers and Rohde, "Turning Out Guerrillas and Terrorists to Wage a Holy War," p. A1.

131. Quoted in Fineman and Braun, "Life Inside Al-Qaeda," p. A1.

132. Quoted in Beyer, "The Most Wanted Man in the World," p. 54.

133. Quoted in C.J. Chivers, "Millions of Afghan Children, and No Ideas About Their Future," *New York Times*, December 4, 2001, p. B1.

134. Quoted in *Time International*, "The Child Soldiers," November 12, 2001, p. 50.

135. Jeffrey Goldberg, "The Education of a Holy Warrior," *New York Times Magazine*, June 25, 1999, p. 32.

136. Goldberg, "The Education of a Holy Warrior," p. 32.

137. Quoted in Goldberg, "The Education of a Holy Warrior," p. 32.

138. Quoted in Goldberg, "The Education of a Holy Warrior," p. 32.

139. Dexter Filkins, "The Legacy of the Taliban Is a Sad and Broken Land," *New York Times*, December 31, 2003, p.A1.

140. Quoted in Filkins, "The Legacy of the Taliban Is a Sad and Broken Land," p. A1.

141. Quoted in Kathy Gannon, "US Forces Sift Al-Qaeda Training Camp," Associated Press, January 3, 2002. www.multimedia.belointeractive.com.

142. Quoted in Bearak, "An Afghan Quilt of Misery," p. A1.

143. Quoted in Hannah Bloch, "A Land of Endless Tears," *Time*, September 24, 2001, p. 59.

Chapter 7: Resistance to the Taliban

144. Ward, "Behind the Veil of Terror," p. 46.

145. Quoted in Ward, "Behind the Veil of Terror," p. 46.

146. Quoted in Barry Bearak, "This Job Is Truly Scary: The Taliban Are Watching," *New York Times*, June 1, 2001, p. A4.

147. Quoted in Bearak, "This Job Is Truly Scary," p. A4.

148. Quoted in Bearak, "This Job Is Truly Scary," p. A4.

149. Quoted in Roddy Scott, "Against All Odds," *Middle East*, April 1999, p. 45.

150. Quoted in Scott, "Against All Odds," p. 45.

151. Quoted in Luke Harding, "Inside Afghanistan's Secret Schools," *Guardian Unlimited*, July 2, 2001. www.guardian.co.uk.

152. Quoted in Harding, "Inside Afghanistan's Secret Schools."

153. Quoted in Norimitsu Onishi, "Medical Schools Show First Signs of Healing from Taliban," *New York Times*, January 15, 2002, p. A12.

154. Quoted in Mackay, "On Seeing the Face of an Afghan Woman."

155. Quoted in Rone Tempest, "Training Camp of Another Kind," *Los Angeles Times*, October 15, 2001, p. A1.

156. Quoted in Armstrong, *Veiled Threat*, p. 157.

157. Quoted in Mackay, "On Seeing the Face of an Afghan Woman."

158. Quoted in Mackay, "On Seeing the Face of an Afghan Woman."

159. Janelle Brown, "The Taliban's Bravest Opponents," *Guardian Unlimited*, October 2, 2001. www.dir.salon.com.

160. Quoted in Mackay, "On Seeing the Face of an Afghan Woman."

161. Junger, *Fire*, p. 212.

162. Quoted in Anthony Davis, "One Less Weapon Against bin Laden," *Time Asia*, September 24, 2001, n.p.

163. Sebastian Junger, "Requiem for a Warrior," *National Geographic Adventure*, November/December 2001, p. 172.

164. Quoted in Armstrong, *Veiled Threat*, p. 164.

165. Quoted in Tempest, "Training Camp of Another Kind," p. A1.

For Further Reading

Books

Laurel Corona, *Afghanistan.* San Diego: Lucent, 2002. Excellent economic and historical information are provided in this book, especially on the effects of the Great Game. A helpful index and bibliography are also included.

Mitch Frank, *Understanding September 11th: Answering Questions About the Attacks on America.* New York: Viking, 2002. This source offers good information on extremist Islam and the terror network of Bin Laden.

Alex Woolf, *Osama bin Laden.* Minneapolis: Lerner, 2004. This easy-to-read book offers good biographical information on Osama bin Laden's early years in Saudi Arabia.

Video

National Geographic, *Afghanistan Revealed.* Clifton, NJ: National Geographic, 2001. Excellent images are presented in this video, including footage of Massoud and his guerrilla fighters as well as life in a refugee camp.

Web Sites

Afghanistan Online (www.afghan-web.com). This site contains a wealth of information about the country—from history and interesting facts about geography to news and popular culture in Afghanistan.

Revolutionary Association of the Women of Afghanistan (RAWA) (www.rawa.org). Originally an underground organization supporting women's rights and documenting the abuse of women during Taliban rule in Afghanistan, RAWA attracted the support of prominent Westerners, who publicized the plight and cause of Afghan women. The site is filled with information about RAWA's history and volunteers, and vivid narratives are supported by photographs. A warning alerts visitors to the site that some of its photographs are graphic and possibly upsetting.

Works Consulted

Books

Sally Armstrong, *Veiled Threat: The Hidden Power of the Women of Afghanistan.* New York: Four Walls Eight Windows, 2002. This book provides excellent interviews of Afghan women and their impressions of life under the rule of the Taliban.

Larry Goodson, *Afghanistan's Endless War: State Failure, Regional Politics, and the Rise of the Taliban.* Seattle: University of Washington Press, 2001. This book includes an excellent index and a very complete glossary.

S. Amjad Hussain, *The Taliban and Beyond: A Close Look at the Afghan Nightmare.* Perrysburg, OH: BWD, 2001. The author offers very readable sections on Afghanistan's recent history as well as information on how the Taliban is structured.

Sebastian Junger, *Fire.* New York: W.W. Norton, 2001. Junger includes a highly readable chapter describing life with Ahmad Shah Massoud, leader of the anti-Taliban Northern Alliance.

Robert D. Kaplan, *Soldiers of God: With Islamic Warriors in Afghanistan and Pakistan.* New York: Vintage Departures, 2001. This book provides an excellent chapter on the prevalence and danger of land mines in Afghanistan.

Latifa, *My Forbidden Face: Growing Up Under the Taliban: A Young Woman's Story.* New York: Hyperion, 2001. A moving first-person account of a teenager who experienced the Taliban's sharia.

Ralph H. Magnus and Eden Naby, *Afghanistan: Mullah, Marx, and Mujahid.* Boulder, CO: Westview, 2002. The authors provide very helpful material concerning the economic problems resulting from the Soviet occupation as well as the civil war in Afghanistan.

William Maley, ed., *Fundamentalism Reborn? Afghanistan and the Taliban.* New York: New York University Press, 2001. Though its reading level is advanced, this book offers excellent details of the political events leading to the emergence of the Taliban.

Kamal Matinuddin, *The Taliban Phenomenon: Afghanistan, 1994–1997.* Oxford, UK: Oxford University Press, 1999. Although difficult reading, this book offers excellent details on the Taliban's rise to power.

Ahmed Rashid, *Taliban: Militant Islam, Oil, and Fundamentalism in Central Asia.* New Haven, CT: Yale University Press, 2002. Although it is somewhat difficult reading, this book includes a very helpful section on the historical background of the Taliban.

Rosemarie Skaine, *The Women of Afghanistan Under the Taliban.* Jefferson, NC: McFarland, 2002. A very readable account of life under the Taliban, including fascinating interviews of a variety of Afghan women.

Batya Swift Yasgur, *Behind the Burqa: Our Life in Afghanistan and How We Escaped to Freedom.* Hoboken, NJ: John Wiley & Sons, 2002. A very readable account of two young women's lives during the time of the civil war and the Taliban government.

Zoya, with John Follain and Rita Cristofari, *Zoya's Story: An Afghan Woman's Struggle for Freedom*. New York: William Morrow, 2002. An excellent first-person account of the Taliban takeover.

Periodicals

Christiane Amanpour, "Tyranny of the Taliban," *Time*, October 13, 1997.

Scott Baldauf, "Afghan Path," *Christian Science Monitor*, April 9, 2001.

———, "Inside a Taliban Terrorism Class," *Christian Science Monitor*, May 6, 2003.

Barry Bearak, "An Afghan Mosaic of Misery," *New York Times*, February 25, 2000.

———, "Afghans Ruled by Taliban: Poor, Isolated, but Secure," *New York Times*, October 10, 1998.

———, "This Job Is Truly Scary: The Taliban Are Watching," *New York Times*, June 1, 2001.

Chris de Bellaique, "When the Price of Security Is a Life of Poverty," *Independent*, January 10, 2001.

Lisa Beyer, "The Most Wanted Man in the World," *Time*, September 24, 2001.

Hannah Bloch, "A Land of Endless Tears," *Time*, September 24, 2001.

Bloomington Pantagraph (IL), "In Afghanistan, Head-to-Toe Garment Hides Identity, Outrage," October 30, 1996.

Chicago Tribune, "In the Name of Islam, Couple Stoned to Death," November 3, 1996.

C.J. Chivers, "Millions of Afghan Children, and No Ideas About Their Future," *New York Times*, December 4, 2001.

———, "Veterans of Soviets' Old War Warn of Betrayal and Brutality," *New York Times*, October 22, 2001.

C.J. Chivers and David Rohde, "Turning Out Guerrillas and Terrorists to Wage a Holy War," *New York Times*, March 18, 2002.

Pam Constable, "Afghanistan Struggling to Rebuild," *Washington Post*, October 3, 1993.

Current Events, "Storm From the Hills," November 4, 1996.

John-Thor Dahlberg, "Afghan Orphans Face a Pitiless Future," *Los Angeles Times*, November 3, 1996, p. A1.

Anthony Davis, "One Less Weapon Against bin Laden," *Time Asia*, September 24, 2001.

Debra Denker, "Along Afghanistan's War-Torn Frontier," *National Geographic*, June 1985.

Erik Eckholm, "Taliban Justice: Stadium Was Scene of Gory Punishment," *New York Times*, December 26, 2001.

Abbas Faiz, "Health Care Under the Taliban," *Lancet*, April 26, 1997.

Dexter Filkins, "The Legacy of the Taliban Is a Sad and Broken Land," *New York Times*, December 31, 2003.

———, "Under Autumn Snow, Footnotes to Village's Sorrowful Decade," *New York Times*, December 9, 2001.

Mark Fineman and Stephen Braun, "Life Inside Al-Qaeda: A Destructive Devotion," *Los Angeles Times*, September 24, 2001.

Carlotta Gall, "Killings from Taliban's Era Still Haunt a Valley," *New York Times*, July 25, 2002.

Jeffrey Goldberg, "The Education of a Holy Warrior," *New York Times Magazine*, June 25, 1999.

Human Rights Watch, "The Massacre in Mazar-i Sharif," vol. 10, November 1998.

Scott Johnson, "Love Under the Taliban," *Newsweek International*, April 1, 2002.

Sebastian Junger, "Requiem for a Warrior," *National Geographic Adventure*, November/December 2001.

Shugofa Noori Kabir, "Cloaked in Danger,"

Teen Magazine, August 1999.

Marc Kaufman, "Afghan Rules in the Strictest Sense," Knight-Ridder/Tribune News Service, October 12, 1996.

Nadya Labi, "Rhythmless Nation," *Time*, September 15, 2001.

Mavis Leno, "The World Needs to Know the Awful Plight of Afghan Women," *Chicago Tribune*, November 1, 1998.

Michael Lev, "Holy War Without End," *Chicago Tribune*, November 24, 1996.

———, "Tyranny of Religion Imperils Rich Culture," *Chicago Tribune*, December 3, 1996.

Emily MacFarquhar, "The Rise of Taliban: A New Force of Muslim Fighters Is Determined to Rule Afghanistan," *U.S. News & World Report*, March 6, 1995.

Ian MacWilliam, "Afghan Villagers Feel Betrayed by Taliban Zealots," *Plain Dealer*, November 8, 1996.

Johanna McGeary, "The Taliban Troubles," *Time*, October 1, 2001.

Andrew Meier, "Stoners," "*New Republic*, October 7, 1996.

Norimitsu Onishi, "Medical Schools Show First Signs of Healing from Taliban," *New York Times*, January 15, 2002.

Katha Pollitt, "Tearing at the Veil," *New York Times Magazine*, May 14, 2000.

John Rettie, "Afghan Trail Open Only to VIPs, Liars, and Inspectors," *Manchester Guardian*, August 27, 1993.

Roddy Scott, "Against All Odds," *Middle East*, April 1999.

Amir Shah, "Afghan Refugees Swamp Pakistan Border," *San Diego Union-Tribune*, November 29, 2000.

Radek Sikorski, "Killing Time: Kabul, Afghanistan," *Times* (London), September 25, 1993.

Anthony Spaeth, "A Peace That Terrifies," *Time*, October 14, 1996.

Sunday Mirror, "The West at War," September 30, 2001.

Diane Taylor, "Real Lives," *Daily Mirror*, March 24, 2001.

Rone Tempest, "Training Camp of Another Kind," *Los Angeles Times*, October 15, 2001.

Time, "About Face," December 3, 2001.

———, "Frozen in Time," May 29, 2000.

Time International, "The Child Soldiers," November 12, 2001.

———, "End of the Line," February 26, 2001.

USA Today, "US Expected to Target Afghanistan's Opium," October 16, 2001.

Amy Waldman, "No TV, No Chess, No Kites," *New York Times*, November 22, 2001.

Wall Street Journal, "Divided Front?" October 1, 2001.

Amanda Ward, "Behind the Veil of Terror," *Daily Mirror*, June 21, 2001.

Peter Willems, "Afghanistan's Gold," *Middle East*, September 1997.

———, "Principles at a Price," *Middle East*, March 1997.

———, "War Without End," *Middle East*, December 1996.

Kim Willsher, "Prisoners of the Burqa," *Times* (London), October 5, 2001.

Internet Sources

Janelle Brown, "The Taliban's Bravest Opponents," *Guardian Unlimited*, October 2, 2001. www.dir.salon.com.

Kathy Gannon, "US Forces Sift Al-Qaeda Training Camp," Associated Press, January 3, 2002. www.multimedia.belointeractive.com.

Luke Harding, "Inside Afghanistan's Secret Schools," *Guardian Unlimited*, July 2, 2001. www.guardian.co.uk.

Khalid Hasan, "The Taliban's World," *Hindunet*. March 19, 2001. www.hvk.org.

Sijida Hayat, "Kabul: The City Where Even

the Sunrise and Sunset Have Been Upset for a Long Time," *RAWA Online*, January 2000. www.rawa.org.

Tim Judah, "Profile: Mullah Mohammad Omar," *Guardian Unlimited Observer*, September 23, 2001. www.observer.co.uk.

Christina Lamb, "I Was One of the Taliban's Torturers," *London Telegraph Online*, September 30, 2001. www.telegraph. co.uk.

————, "Taliban Bring Terror to Refugee Camps," *London Telegraph Online*, September 30, 2001. www.telegraph.co.uk.

Leslie Mackay, "On Seeing the Face of an Afghan Woman," *Moxie Magazine Online*, 2001. www.moxiemag.com.

Pankaj Mishra, "The Making of Afghanistan," *New York Review of Books*, November 15, 2001. www.nybooks.com.

Charles H. Norchi, "Blowback from Afghanistan: The Historical Roots," *ciaonet*, February 1996. www.ciaonet.org.

PBS Frontline, "Trail of a Terrorist." www. pbs.org.

John Sifton, "A Last Road Trip Through Pre-modern Afghanistan," *Peace Pledge Union*, September 30, 2001. www.ppu. org.uk.

Index

secret codes of, 73
see also training camps

Rahmad, Nessar, 56
Rashid, Ahmed, 12
Reagan, Ronald, 19
refugee camps
  Khaiwa (RAWA camp) and,
    85–86
  in Pakistan, 19, 21, 23, 28,
    65
  poverty in, 62–64
refugees
  people smugglers and, 65–66
  al Qaeda and, 76
  U.S. war on terror and, 91
relief agencies, 57, 59–60, 62,
  64, 79
"Requiem for a Warrior"
  (Junger), 89
Ressam, Ahmed, 74
Revolutionary Association of
  the Women of Afghanistan
  (RAWA), 84–88
Rohde, David, 72
Rubenstein, Leonard, 46
Russia, 13

Saba, Sehar (fictitious RAWA
  name), 86
Saudi Arabia, 20, 30, 68–69, 76
September 11, 2001, 90–91
Shah, Saira, 87–88
sharia. *See* Islamic law
Shomali plain (Afghanistan), 33
Sifton, John, 62, 64
Sikorski, Radek, 26–27
Skaine, Rosemarie, 31, 47
Soldiers of God: With Islamic
  Warriors in Afghanistan and
  Pakistan (Kaplan), 17
Somalia, 69
Soviet Union
  Cold War and, 19
  communism and, 15–16
  flag of, 15

Special Course in Terrorism,
  72
Stingers (surface-to-air
  missiles), 20, 26
"Stoners" (Meier), 34
Sudan, 69, 76
Supreme Shura, 35
Syria, 20

Tajikistan, 28
Tajiks (Afghan tribe), 12
Taliban
  bin Laden and, 69–71,
    78–79
  brutality of, 10, 31, 42–43
  Buddha statues and, 78–79
  ethnic minorities and, 31–33
  financial support of, 30
  government experience of,
    56
  origin of, 27–30
  Pashtuns and, 28, 33
  poppy production and,
    66–67
  songs of, 37
  students of, 28–29, 39
  Supreme Shura and, 35
  U.S. war on terror and,
    90–91
  see also Taliban laws
"Taliban, O Taliban, You're
  Creating Facilities, You're
  Defeating Enemies" (song),
  37
"Taliban Arrived and True"
  (song), 37
Taliban laws
  art and, 39
  curfew and, 53, 64
  dating and, 41
  description of, 9–10
  "Edict Number One" and, 51
  forbidden activities and, 35,
    38–40, 43, 82
  men's beards and, 35, 37, 43,
    56

music and, 37–39
  prayer time and, 36
  punishments for breaking,
    42–45
  resistance to, 80–88
    documenting atrocities
      and, 86–88
    guerrilla fighters and,
      88–90
    RAWA and, 85–86
    television and, 80–81
    underground beauty
      parlors and, 80
  social customs and, 61–62
  television and, 35, 39, 80
Taliqan (Afghan village), 82
Tanzania, 70
Taraki, Nur Mohammed, 15
Time (magazine), 54
training camps
  children and, 76–78
  covert operations training
    and, 72–73
  establishment of, 69
  explosives and, 74–75
  poisons and, 74
  refugees and, 76
  religion and, 72
  Special Course in Terrorism
    and, 72
  suicide missions and, 75–76
  teaching methods at, 71, 74
Turkmen (nomadic tribe), 12
"Turning Out Guerrillas and
  Terrorists to Wage a Holy
  War" (Chivers and Rohde), 72
Turyalai (Afghan man), 44–45
"Tyranny of the Taliban"
  (Amanpour), 54

United Nations (UN), 23–24,
  64
United States
  Afghanistan anger toward, 79
  bin Laden declaration of
    jihad against, 70

Picture Credits

About the Author

Gail B. Stewart received her undergraduate degree from Gustavus Adolphus College in St. Peter, Minnesota. She did her graduate work in English, linguistics, and curriculum study at the College of St. Thomas and the University of Minnesota. She taught English and reading for more than ten years.

She has written over ninety books for young people, including a series for Lucent Books called The Other America. She has written many books on historical topics such as World War I and the Warsaw ghetto.

Stewart and her husband live in Minneapolis with their three sons, Ted, Elliot, and Flynn; two dogs; and a cat. When she is not writing, she enjoys reading, walking, and watching her sons play soccer.